THE SEARCH

THE SEARCH

The Soul's Secret Signature

R. Wayne Stacy

R. W. Stacy

FIELDS PUBLISHING INC.
NASHVILLE, TENNESSEE

Printed in the United States of America

Library of Congress Card Number: 00-106007

ISBN: 1-57843-007-0

P. O. Box 728 • Brentwood, Tennessee 37024
800-966-2278
e-mail:cdeweese@tnbaptist.org

Fields Publishing Inc.
917 Harpeth Valley Place • Nashville, Tennessee 37221
615-662-1344
e-mail: tfields@fieldspublishing.com

In Memory of

J. D. Stacy

*who made my own search for God
a little more like
coming home.*

Contents

Introduction   8

Part One: The Search

Chapter 1   The Search   15
Chapter 2   Metaphor Moments   23
Chapter 3   Glimpses of Glory   29
Chapter 4   Epiphany   35

Part Two: The Sought

Chapter 5   The Hound of Heaven   43
Chapter 6   God on the Gallows   49
Chapter 7   The Moment of Truth   57
Chapter 8   Angels We Have Heard Nearby   63

Part Three: Home

Chapter 9   A Whole New Life   73
Chapter 10   The Presence in the Absence   77
Chapter 11   The Gathering   83
Chapter 12   God's Geography   87

Notes   93
About the Author   96

Introduction

C. S. Lewis once said that human beings are haunted by the fact that we know, and know inchoately, that we were once something much different, much better, than we are now, but that somehow that "something" got lost. By itself that would be bad enough. However, Lewis went on to say that we human beings, having lost that "something," yet retain a memory of what we were and what we lost, a memory that hounds and haunts us. He talked about that sense of being "haunted" often. He called it *Sehnsucht,* or "longing," or "Joy." In *Mere Christianity* he described it thus:

> Most people, if they had really learned to look into their own hearts, would know that they do want, and want acutely, something that cannot be had in this world. There are all sorts of things in this world that offer to give it to you, but they never quite keep their promise. The longings which arise in us when we first fall in love, or first think of some foreign country, or first take up some subject that excites us, are longings which no marriage, no travel, no learning, can really satisfy. There was something we grasped at, in that first moment of longing, which just fades away in the reality. I think everyone knows what I mean.... If I find in myself a desire which no experience in this world can satisfy, the most probable explanation is that I was made for another world.... Probably earthly pleasures were never meant to satisfy it [longing], but only to arouse it, to suggest the real thing. If that is so, I must take care, on the one hand, never to despise, or be unthankful for, these earthly blessings, and on the other, never to mistake them for the something else of which they are only a kind of copy, or echo, or mirage.[1]

In another place he called it "the soul's secret signature."[2] "Your soul," he said, "has a curious shape because it is a hollow made to fit a particular swelling in the infinite contours of the divine substance...."[3] He continued:

> And what shall we take this secrecy to mean? Surely, that each of the redeemed shall forever know and praise some one aspect of the divine beauty better than any other creature can. Why else were individuals created, but that God, loving all infinitely, should love each differently?[4]

So consumed was he with that sense of being haunted by that "something else" that he titled his autobiography *Surprised by Joy,* as though his entire life had been nothing more than a search, sometimes a desperate search, for Joy—and it was! It was the real subject of almost everything he wrote. So convinced was he about this ubiquitous sense of Presence in the absence that he said that when the Great Denouemént unfolded at the end of all things and we behold finally the object of our restless search, we shall not in this Presence be without recognition: "I'm sorry; I don't believe I know you," but shall instead say: "So it was *You* all the time!"[5] Joy—it is our fondest memory; it is our fiercest hope. Indeed, it is the place where memory and hope are virtually indistinguishable, where memory and hope become one.

Lewis was not alone in this. Wordsworth talked about "intimations of immortality." Augustine, whose own autobiography takes the form of a search for God, said that there was a "God-shaped blank" in every person that can only be filled by God, and that each person is restless until s/he should find Him. The search—it is as old as the *Enuma Elish* in which Gilgamesh seeks out wise, old Utnapishtim for assistance in his quest for eternal life. It is the subject of Malory's *Morte D'Arthur,* of Spenser's *Faerie Queene,* of Donne's *Holy Sonnets,* of George MacDonald's *Phantastes,* and of J. R. R. Tolkien's trilogy. It is a theme in sacred and secular literature alike. Of course, if Lewis is correct in his supposition that there is a *universal* longing for God, then the distinction between "secular" and "sacred" seems far less useful. In any case, it figures prominently in literature, in music, and in film. From George Lucas' *Star Wars* to Ron Howard's *Cocoon* to Richard LaGravanese's *The Fisher King,* the search has fascinated film's best storytellers. Billy Joel sings about it in up-tempo, rock rhythms in his song *The River of Dreams*: "I've been searching for something/ Taken out of my soul/ Something I would never lose/ Something somebody stole."[6] It is the story we learned as children, the story with a thousand characters but one plot—the wicked witch worked the evil spell that ruined everything, and the desperate search for the secret that works the spell backwards and sets it all right again. Both in poetry and prose, from the romantic to the contemporary periods, the "search" or the "quest" is a constant theme. William Butler Yeats, especially in his earlier poetry, writes of little else. The poetry of T. S. Eliot is dominated by the imagery of the Grail; sometimes explicit, sometimes implicit, it is never far from his mind. John Steinbeck once said that only two great stories were worth telling: the Cross and the Grail. Both, of course, are ultimately about the "search."

Flannery O'Connor, in commenting on her own work and on the work of her fellow Southern writers, once said that: "By and large people in the

South still conceive of humanity in theological terms. While the South is hardly Christ-centered, it is most certainly Christ-haunted. The Southerner who isn't convinced of it is very much afraid that he may have been formed in the image and likeness of God."[7] One doesn't have to spend much time with Southern fiction to validate her conclusion. From Walker Percy to Reynolds Price to Allan Gurganus, the "search" is the story behind the story.

Perhaps no Christian writer in recent memory has been more influential than Frederick Buechner. A prolific writer of both fiction and non-fiction, the search, typically described by Buechner as the "hunger," is the single most dominant theme of his writing. He once titled a book of his sermons *The Hungering Dark,* and the individual sermon titles tell the tale: "The Face in the Sky," The Calling of Voices," "Come and See," "The Sign by the Highway," "The Killing of Time," "The Rider," "The Hungering Dark." In that last sermon Buechner tells a story about his being in Rome on Christmas Eve for the Papal Mass. He describes in meticulous detail the appearance of the Pope as he emerged to bless the throng assembled for the mass. To Buechner's amazement, the Pope was not gazing causally into the crowd. He was leaning forward, peering intently into that sea of faces, as though he were looking for something, or Someone. Buechner says:

> He was not a potentate nodding and smiling to acknowledge the enthusiasm of the multitudes. He was a man whose face seemed gray with waiting, whose eyes seemed huge and exhausted with searching, for someone, some one, who he thought might be there that night or any night, anywhere, but whom he had never found, and yet he kept looking. Face after face he searched for the face that he knew he would know—was it this one? was it this one? or this one?—and then he passed on out of my sight. It was a powerful moment for me, a moment that many other things have crystallized about since, and I felt that I knew whom he was looking for. I felt that anyone else who was really watching must also have known.[8]

The early church, it seems, was "really watching," for they too were fixated on that "Face." The overriding crisis of the New Testament was the absence of Jesus, and his return, described in the New Testament as his *parousia,* was the object of great hope and longing. The absence of Jesus and the hunger for his return is the dominant theme of much of the New Testament. Virtually every writer in the New Testament feels compelled to address it in one fashion or another. It was the center of their worship when they gathered together. They shared bread and cup in remembrance of Him, and before they scattered they prayed—always the same prayer as though it *had* to be the last word—often in difficulty, frequently in desperation, they prayed *maranatha,* "Our Lord, Come!" It seems that they too were always searching, eyes darting this way and that, for that "Face."

Moreover, the "hunger" is reciprocal. I am both the searcher and the sought, the pursuer and the pursued: God's query, "Adam, where are you?" or Moses commanded to take off his shoes at the Bush, or Samuel awakened by a Voice in the night calling him by name. In G. K. Chesterton's mysterious and marvelous story, *The Man Who Was Thursday*, the protagonist finds himself stalked, by One who's desire for him will neither let him go nor let him off. C. S. Lewis in describing his own journey to God depicts more a flight from God than to God: "You must picture me alone in that room in Magdalen, night after night, feeling, whenever my mind lifted even for a second from my work, the steady, unrelenting approach of Him whom I so earnestly desired not to meet."[9]

In another place Lewis, in distinguishing between Christianity's understanding of God and the Pantheist's, writes:

> The Pantheist's God does nothing, demands nothing. He is there if you wish for Him, like a book on a shelf. He will not pursue you.... If He [Pantheist's God] were the truth, then we could really say that all the Christian images of kingship were a historical accident of which our religion ought to be cleansed. It is with a shock that we discover them to be indispensable. You have had a shock like that before, in connection with smaller matters— when the line pulls at your hand, when something breathes beside you in the darkness.... It is always shocking to meet life where we thought we were alone.... An "impersonal God"—well and good. A subjective God of beauty, truth and goodness, inside our own heads—better still. A formless life-force surging through us, a vast power which we can tap—best of all. But God Himself, alive, pulling at the other end of the cord, perhaps approaching at an infinite speed, the hunter, king, husband— that is quite another matter. There comes a moment when the children who have been playing at burglars hush suddenly: was that a *real* footstep in the hall? There comes a moment when people who have been dabbling in religion ("Man's search for God"!) suddenly draw back. Supposing we really found Him? We never meant it to come to *that*! Worse still, supposing He had found us?[10]

When "hunter" and "hunted" are found (who finds whom first is not really important), the dance of delight is engaged; the party is started; the Joy for which we were made is realized; the bad dream is ended; it is morning, and we are home.

My preaching over the past twenty or so years, I find, has moved me in and out of this theme more than I realized. Typically, I employ the Lectionary in text selection, and so if this preaching on the "search" is contrived it is not intentionally so. Rather, I suspect Steinbeck is right—it is finally the only story worth telling.

I have gathered together in this place my sermonizing on the search, the "hunger"—ours for God, and God's for us. The sermons seem to fall naturally into three categories: The Search (my search for God), The Sought (God's search for me), and Home (my sense of "at-home-ness" with God). I offer them merely as one preacher's attempt to "name the hunger," to "touch the wound," to "see the Face" for which each of us searches in the desperate hope that somehow, some way, someday *we* might be found.

One more word—sermons are situation-specific, an indigenous word of God for a particular people in a particular place at a particular time. These sermons are no exception. They found expression in a pastor's weekly (sometimes weakly) attempt to speak a word of God to the people whom he was called to serve. They are not sermons spoken into the air "to whom it may concern." They are real sermons addressed to real people. Some of those real people who heard a word of God through them have harassed and hassled and hounded me into publication. I resisted doing so, in part because these sermons were "personal words" to my congregations, and in part because these sermons were written for the ear, not for the eye. I wrote them with the pulpit in view, knowing that they would be nestled in worship among the reading of Scripture, the singing of hymns, prayer, confession, communion, and the doxology. To extract them from the context for which they were intended and created seemed to me to be inappropriate. However, after persistent cajoling I offer them now to a reading congregation and ask that, if possible, they at least be read *aloud.*

I also must thank the two congregations for which these sermons were originally prepared and preached: the First Baptist Church of Raleigh, North Carolina, and the First Baptist Church of Shelby, North Carolina. With Paul I can say: "I thank my God every time I think about you."

PART ONE

THE SEARCH

The Search

Amos 6:1-14; Luke 12:13-21

Shel Silverstein has written a haunting little poem in his book *Where The Sidewalk Ends* which he calls "The Search." It is the story of a man in search of the proverbial "pot of gold at the end of the rainbow." After searching high and low for his prize, suddenly, there in the grass, he finds it. Gleefully, he shouts, "It's mine at last!" But then, reality settles over him, and he realizes that that which he thought would be the "be all and end all" wasn't and didn't. With weary resignation he casts his eyes to the horizon in search of the next thing that promises to satiate the gnawing hunger to find "it," whatever "it" turns out to be.[2]

Now, I understand this man! The lure of the discovery of that which will finally make one "secure," the proverbial "pot of gold" at the end of the rainbow, the feeling that one has finally "arrived"—arrived *where* we're not sure, but we know we're not "there" now—can be consuming, literally. Indeed, in antiquity this search is often pictured as a gnawing, insatiable appetite, a "hunger" that cannot be sated.

There's an old, old story, widely traveled, about a hermit who stumbled onto a cave in which there was hidden an enormous treasure. The hermit, being old and wise of years, realized what he had discovered and immediately took to his heels and ran from the cave as fast as he could. As he was running, he came upon three brigands who stopped him and inquired as to what he was fleeing.

"I'm fleeing the Devil!" he said.

Curious, they said: "Show us."

Protesting all the way, he took them to the cave where he had found the treasure.

"Here," said the hermit, "is death which was running after me."

Well, the three thought the old man was touched and sent him on his way. Gleefully reveling in their new-found treasure, they determined that one of them should be dispatched to bring back provisions, lest they leave their treasure to others. One volunteered, thinking to himself that while in town, he'd poison the food and kill his rivals possessing the treasure for himself. But while he was away, the other two had been thinking too! They decided to kill their comrade when he returned and divide the spoils between them. This they did and settled down to eat their food and celebrate their successful cabal. But their banquet turned out to be a funeral feast, for when the poison hit their stomachs, they too expired, leaving the treasure as they had found it.

That's one of the oldest pictures of greed we have. It lurks in caves; it deals in death.

But the search goes on, and the hunger is unabated. Like a man looking for the market where life is sold, we run all over town with a fist full of twenty dollar bills saying, "Hey, could I buy a...."

"No, sorry, we don't sell homes here. We can sell you a *house.*"

"No, sorry, we don't sell love here. We can sell you a *companion* for the night."

"No, sorry, we don't sell any time. I got a good clock here, but not a *tick of time.*"

The lure of the "search" can be consuming. That elusive goal of "financial independence" got millions to watch the halftime of the Super Bowl recently. No, Elvis was not performing. Rather, the draw was Ed McMahon and Dick Clark cruising America in the Publisher's Clearing House Prize Patrol van looking for the house where they would make someone an instant millionaire. The prize would be awarded on live TV during halftime of the Super Bowl, and millions of Americans were peering out their windows saying: "Mildred, is that a van I see coming down our street?"

It's not a new phenomenon. Israel was engaged in such a "search" in the eighth century B. C. when the prophet Amos came along and called the whole enterprise into question.

It was the "Silver Age" of Israel during the reign of Jeroboam II when the "search" began in earnest. Under Jeroboam Israel enjoyed nearly unparalleled prosperity, power, and prestige. Jeroboam's military conquests had expanded the frontiers to a point where Israel's holdings nearly rivaled those of the great Davidic monarchy. "From the entrance of Hamath to the Brook of the Arabah" was the proud slogan of the day. Here in North Carolina we say "from Manteo to Murphy." You get the idea. In order to further secure this new expansionism, Jeroboam negotiated a series of alliances with foreign powers, chiefly Assyria, and the resulting *pax Jeroboam* gave rise to unparalleled trade and commerce in Israel.

Israel enjoyed "the good life" under Jeroboam, and the affluent upper class who were the chief beneficiaries of this unprecedented economic and military security celebrated their good fortune with "conspicuous consumption," flaunting an opulent lifestyle that included garish banquets and endless revelry. Under Jeroboam Israel had "arrived," there was "ease in Zion" and "security in Samaria."

But this was not true for everyone. Israel's poor, working class did not share in the blessings of the rich, and the gap between the "haves" and the "have nots" grinned ghoulishly. Enter Amos. Railing at the injustice and exploitation of Israel's wealthy against the poor, Amos hurled defiant words in the face of the "notable men of the first of the nations."

"You who trample the poor and take from him exactions of wheat... who afflict the righteous, who take bribes, and turn aside the needy in the gate.... Thus saith the LORD, the God of hosts, I will pass through your midst, and it's not for a social call..." or words to that effect.

It's not merely a "redistribution of wealth" Amos is after; Israel's problem is more basic than that. "Woe to you who are at ease in Zion, and to those who *feel* secure on the mountain of Samaria...for you shall be first to go into exile, and the revelry of those who stretch themselves [on banquet couches] shall pass away."

Israel's problem is not just greed or even exploitation of their fellow Israelites, as bad as that is; it's the fact that they've attempted to secure themselves *apart from God!* It is not wealth *per se* that's the problem. If it were, then merely redistributing the wealth from the rich to the poor would solve nothing and would, in fact, work to the detriment of the poor, making them the new recipients of the "evil stuff."

Nothing is necessarily or intrinsically evil in wealth anymore than anything is necessarily or intrinsically virtuous in poverty. People of wealth or poverty can be either saints or sinners, but nothing in their economic status *per se* makes them so. As C. S. Lewis has put it: "Evil is a parasite." That is, evil has no *independent* life. Everything bad is something *essentially* good that has been bent, misshapen, twisted toward some inappropriate end. The biblical perspective is that God created all things and pronounced them "good." No, it's not merely a redistribution of wealth with which Amos is concerned. He has "bigger fish to fry" than that!

Now don't misunderstand me. I'm not saying that "rich" and "poor" are the same, only *relative*. I remind you, by the *world's* standards everyone reading this page is "rich." The vast majority of the citizens of this country step on scales every day. The biggest single "party affiliation" in this country is neither Democrat nor Republican; it's "Weight Watchers," a problem most of the world couldn't understand. Amos never in his wildest dreams envisioned a world where the quality of life even remotely approached the one you and I enjoy. That's not what he meant.

I'm not saying that we shouldn't care about *economic* justice. In a "world without borders" anyone anywhere starving is my neighbor starving! But a Jeremiad (perhaps I should say "Amosiad") against the "rich," always careful to define "rich" as someone other than me, hardly does justice to the prophet's words.

It's the idolatry of treating as an end that which was originally intended to be merely a means that Amos has in mind—"Woe to those at ease in Zion and secure in Samaria." St. Augustine once put it this way: "We enjoy those things that were meant only to be used, and we use those things that were meant to be enjoyed." We go through life getting our advanced degrees, earning our salaries, driving our cars, paying our mortgages, believing all the while that this establishes who we *really* are, only to be reminded when we least expect it what we've always known—that we're all just a stroke or a tumor away from finding out who we *really* are.

One of my favorite movies was a story called *Julia*. It was the story about a friendship between a woman named Julia and the famous playwright Lillian Hellman.

My favorite scene in the movie occurred one night when Lillian Hellman, played by Jane Fonda in the movie, was sitting out by the fire on the beach talking with her literary mentor, Dashiell Hammett, creator of the "Sam Spade" character and author of such mystery novels as *The Maltese Falcon* and *The Thin Man*, played by Jason Robards in the movie. Lillian had just published her first play, her famous *The Little Foxes,* and was for the first time realizing some fame and financial independence.

Sitting there by the firelight, thoughts of greatness fluttered in her head, and she turned to Dashiell Hammett and said: "Dash, do you think it would be frivolous of me to buy a mink coat with some of the money from my play? You know, I've never had much money, and I've always wanted a mink coat. I can just imagine walking into one of those posh New York writers' parties, all the big names there, wearing my new mink and having everyone in the place turn in chorus, look at me and say: 'Why, that's Lillian Hellman. She's somebody!'"

And Hammett, stirring around in the coals, never looking at her, says: "Lilly, if you want a coat, buy a coat. God knows you've got the money now; but don't think for a moment that it has anything to do with writing. It's just a coat, Lilly. That's all. Just a coat."

The problem with wealth is not that it's *intrinsically* evil; it's that it seduces us into thinking that it can give what only God can give— security.

You recall the man rather unceremoniously remembered in the New Testament as "The Rich Fool?" A rich farmer had a better-than-expected harvest. So consumed was he with his good fortune that his biggest problem was where to store all his "stuff." Resourceful, he decided to dismantle his meager barns and construct in their place super, giant-sized grain silos in which to store his "security." Having done so, he's convinced that finally, *finally,* he's secure in his wealth, that his "ship has come in." He says to himself: "Self, relax. Take it easy. You've got it made. It's Easy Street for you from now on." God comes to him that night and says: "You fool, tonight you're going to 'buy the farm' (pardon the pun), and you won't even be around to watch your children argue over their inheritance!"

Isn't that the way you heard the story? The moral of the story is: "You can't take it with you." "No U-Hauls behind a hearse."

We didn't need Jesus to tell us that! There's got to be more here than that! When you read the story carefully, there is.

The key to Jesus' meaning is in the correct translation of verse 20. Most translations render it: "Fool! This night your soul is required of you; and the things you've prepared, whose will they be?" But that's not what Jesus said. In the Greek, the subject of the sentence is not "your soul" but *"they."* Jesus actually said: "You Fool, this night *they* shall require from you your very life; now, who owns whom?"

The question is: Who is *"they?"* The answer, of course, is the *things*—all the "stuff" the rich man had been so concerned about that he had to build bigger barns to hold it all.

Don't you see? *He didn't die!* That's not Jesus' point. Jesus' point is: All that "stuff" you thought you owned *owns you!* You've got to protect it, take care of it, keep people from stealing it, spend sleepless nights wondering where to store it—you don't own *it*; it owns *you*! It's not security it brings you; just the *illusion* of security. Stuff can never give you that. Only *God* can!

When the question is "Life," the answer is "God!" Nothing, and I mean *nothing* else can satisfy "The Search." Everything else is a fraud!

That was Israel's problem, and in the nearly 2,800 intervening years, it's surprising how little has changed. We still think it's possible to secure ourselves apart from God, but just like Israel's hollow hubris in its economic and political and military clout, all our efforts at "independence" from God only serve to demonstrate just how impotent we are without him. The reason is not difficult to see—we were made not just *by* God but *for* God. He's the "fuel" on which we were designed to run, and should we try to run our lives on anything else, like Israel, we discover that it'll never work.

"Do horses run upon rocks? Does one plow the sea with oxen?"

To reject our absolute dependence on God in the search for security is to cut the cord that alone gives us our very lives. To find our security in anything other than our trust in God is not "salvation," it's "damnation!"

Can you imagine Shakespeare's character Hamlet stopping in the middle of Shakespeare's famous play and saying: "All right, all right, Will. I get the idea. I'll take it from here. I don't need you to write lines for me anymore." Would Hamlet thereby have discovered his "true selfhood"? Of course not! That would not be Hamlet's "salvation"; it would be his "destruction." For Hamlet, Prince of Denmark, only exists in the creative imagination of William Shakespeare, and to seek to find his identity outside of and apart from that relationship is self-destruction.

So it is with you and me. *We were made for God.* He "thought us up" like characters in a play. There is no life, no security outside of that life-giving relationship with him. In the Old Testament we call that "covenant." In the New Testament we call it "gospel." Call it what you will, it's a "wake-up call."

Hear Amos: "Nothing—not wealth, not power, not position—*Lo-debar, no-thing* can supply what you really seek. Because what you want, what you *really* want, only God can give."

Centuries after Amos, Blaise Pascal, in his *Pensées* (257), reminded us that there are three kinds of people: those who have sought God and found Him, and these are reasonable and happy; those who seek God and have not yet found him, and these are reasonable and unhappy; and those who neither seek God nor find Him, and these are unreasonable and unhappy.

Fred Craddock, retired professor of preaching at the Candler School of Theology at Emory University, tells a story about playing Hide and Seek as a child. They lived on a farm and didn't have much money. Hide and Seek didn't cost anything, and it was something the kids could play.

You know how the game goes. Someone is "It." Whoever is "It" has to hide their eyes and count to one hundred while everyone else runs and hides. When they get to one hundred, they say, "Here I come, ready or not." Then the person who is "It" looks high and low for those who have hidden. When he finds one, he says, "I found you!" and races back to "home base," usually a tree or something, tags it three times, and then that person becomes "It," and the game starts all over again. Simple.

Well, when Craddock's sister was "It," she cheated. Oh, she'd start out honest enough, "One, two, three, four." Then, when she thought no one was watching, she'd skip a bunch of numbers: "ninety-seven, ninety-eight, ninety-nine, one hundred. Here I come, ready or not!"

But Craddock had a way to beat her. He was much younger and smaller, and so he had a favorite place to hide where she couldn't find him. It was under the front porch steps. It was such a tight squeeze no one else would even try it, but because he was so little, he could do it.

"Ninety-seven, ninety-eight, ninety-nine, one hundred; here I come, ready or not!" Out she went across the yard, out in the back, in the barn, out of the barn, in the corn crib, she couldn't find him! She looked everywhere! Once, she got close to the steps. Craddock thought she'd found him, but she just sat down on the steps to rest, right over the top of where he was hiding. He started giggling; thought he'd give it away, but he didn't.

He thought to himself: "She'll never find me. She'll never find me."
Then it occurred to him: "She'll *never* find me!"

So he stuck out a toe. She came by the steps, saw his toe and said:
"Uh oh, I found you!" ran back to the tree, touched it three times, and
said: "You're it!"

Craddock came out from under the steps, brushed off his clothes, and
said: "Ah shucks! You *found* me!"

Now, why would he do that? What did he want? What did he *really*
want?

The very same thing as *you*. Isn't that true...?

CHAPTER TWO

Metaphor Moments

John 17:1-26

Back in 1985 I resigned my faculty position at the college in Florida at which I was teaching at the time to assume a similar position at Midwestern Baptist Theological Seminary in Kansas City, Missouri. The movers had come and emptied our house, and so Cheryl, Justin, myself, and our cocker spaniel, Quincy, were left to make the 1,300-mile trek north to Kansas City. In addition to the family car, we owned a small boat at the time and an old, beat-up Datsun pickup truck. Thinking the old truck to be unable to pull the boat, we decided that Cheryl would pull the boat with the car, and I would drive the old truck. So early one hot, August morning my little family set out for Kansas City, Quincy and I in the non-air-conditioned pickup truck and Cheryl and Justin in the cool, comfortable, quiet automobile.

For most of the first day, Quincy and I had a high old time. Well, at least I did. I talked to him and sang to him, anything to pass the time. Quincy just kept looking at me (actually he only *appeared* to be looking at me; he had been blind since he was a puppy) but he kept looking up, panting in the heat, as if to say: "How'd I get stuck in this truck with you?"

Then, on the by-pass in Atlanta, it happened! The rear end gears in the old truck just gave out, and the entire drive train locked up. Fortunately, it happened right at an exit, and so crossing five lanes of traffic I limped onto the exit ramp with my old, crippled truck motioning to Cheryl and Justin in the car behind me to follow me; but hand signals are notoriously difficult to interpret with precision. Cheryl thought I was motioning for her to go on, assuming that I would catch up with her, and so she waved at me and went on by!

Well, there we were, Quincy and I. It was noon on the twelfth of August in the middle of "Hotlanta," and we were stuck on the side of a busy interstate with a truck that wouldn't budge. It was hot, too! I learned later that they set a record in Atlanta that day, 105 degrees.

I looked at Quincy and said: "Don't worry; they'll be back." He kind of whimpered and then started panting again. I got out of the truck and walked over to the overpass so I could see them when they came back to see about us. After about five minutes I said to myself: "Hmm, Cheryl must have had to drive quite a ways to get to the next exit, but she'll be back." After about thirty minutes had passed, I couldn't help it, my male chauvinism bubbled up and I thought to myself: "Women drivers. I can't believe it's taken her this long to find an exit and turn around and come back for me!" I still wasn't worried, actually. I knew she'd be back.

An hour later, I was getting worried. "What if *she's* had car trouble!" "Oh no," I thought, "my poor wife broken down on the side of the road, and I can't help at all!" Then I thought: "Wait a minute. What if she's *not* broken down! What if she saw this as her big chance! She's been telling me for months that she doesn't want to go to Kansas City! Maybe she's decided to seize the opportunity and take off with our son, just the two of them, and start a new life for themselves! In a flash I could see it all. She'd turned left at Atlanta and was heading to L.A. to start over again, and all I got was a broken down truck and a blind cocker spaniel!"

Five hours passed! I had a small thermos of cold water to drink which I'd been sharing with Quincy. (Did I mention it was hot?) We were down to our last cup of water. I poured it in my cup and started to drink it, and Quincy growled at me, so I gave it to him.

Then it hit me like a flash out of the blue. Cheryl would call home and see if I had called and talked with my father. I walked over to a phone booth a few blocks away and called my father back in Florida. The phone rang, he answered, and I said: "Dad?" He said: "Wayne?" Then he said: "Are you guys already there?" I said: "No Dad, not exactly." Then I sheepishly asked: "Uh, by the way, Dad, have you heard from Cheryl?" "What? You mean she's not with you?" I said, "Well, not exactly." Then I told him the whole story. When he had finally stopped laughing, he said he would tell her where I was if she called. I gave him the phone number of the phone booth where I was and told him to give it to Cheryl so we could stay in touch. Finally, finally, she called. Just as I *knew* she would (I know my wife, you see, and she knows me), she called my father, and he told her about me and where I was and how I was and just what I needed. He became my "presence" in my absence. Shortly afterwards, she called and I "talked her in." We left the truck in Atlanta being repaired, and the four of us resumed our journey to Kansas City, though I noticed that Quincy sat as far away from me as possible for the rest of the drive.

It's a frightening thing to be left behind, isn't it? Indeed, even our language of leave-taking reflects the fact that departure meant something so painful, so threatening, that we needed God's help to do it. The English *good-bye*, the Spanish *adios*, the French *adieu* all imply that when we part, in the moment between here and not here, between presence and absence, we'd best give someone to God when we can no longer hold them ourselves. Good-bye. "God be with ye." "Parting is such...sorrow."

It's not at all surprising that when Jesus gathers his disciples together in John's Gospel and tells them that he's leaving and that they're going to be left behind, it takes him five chapters, count 'em, five chapters, to do it—John 13-17. "A little while, and you will see me no more." It is *the* problem in this Gospel—Jesus, the one who called us, taught us, turned water into wine and raised the dead, is *leaving* us. The disciples, says John, are like children playing in the floor, suddenly noticing that mom and dad have put on hat and coat and are about to leave. The questions they ask of Jesus are the same questions: Where are you going? Can we go too? Who's gonna stay with us?

What he does in response to their fear over his impending absence is to *pray* for them. He picks up the phone and "talks to the Father" about them, reassuring them that even when he's gone and no longer with them, if he's talking to the Father and they're talking to the Father, then in a real sense, he's still with them. It becomes in John a "metaphor moment," one of those breakthrough moments when another world, another time, transcendence itself, is pulled like a blanket over ordinary time and ordinary history and which from time-to-time "spikes down" through it, revealing itself and thereby transforming the ordinary into the extraordinary.

In a real sense, not just Jesus' prayers, but his whole life and ministry were in a way a figure of speech, a metaphor, for God. "He who has seen me has seen the Father." "I pray that they may know that everything thou hast given me is from thee!" To be sure, God took on a more palpable, tactile form with the presence of Jesus of Nazareth, but "in a little while," he says, "you will see me no more."

Even in the absence there are those moments, those "metaphor moments," when the presence breaks through, reminding us, reassuring us that "everything thou hast given me is from thee."

Prayer is one of those "metaphor moments." John knew that *the* crisis of the Early Church was the absence of Jesus. It's all well and good for Jesus to be crucified and resurrected and to ascend to the Father, but what of us? Should we look for another to lead us? Do we pick up where he left off? It's great that Jesus gets to return to the Father, but *we* have to remain here! "And now I am no more in the world, but *they are in the world.*"

It wasn't just Jesus' immediate disciples who were concerned about this. What about *future* generations of disciples who never knew Jesus personally or heard him speak or saw him perform miracles—what of them? Is there a word for them too? To reassure not only Jesus' immediate disciples, but also those who would come after, that they would not be "orphaned" by the Departing Christ, John let both them *and us* "overhear" Jesus praying for us. "I do not pray for these only, but also for those who believe in me through their world." That's us! He's talking about us! Jesus is talking to the Father about *you and me!*

Patricia, a chaplain friend of mine who ministers at a retirement community, told some of us at her ordination about an experience she had with some of her residents where she works. She admitted to us that depression was a real factor in her work in that so many of the people she comes to know and love end up dying. She said: "Sometimes I get so depressed that I think I just can't face another day of this, I just can't bear to lose another friend."

Then she said something I found very interesting. She said: "But then I remember that from time to time these precious people say to me, 'Patricia, I'm praying for you,' and I think about that. They've prayed for me, talked to God *about me!* I remember that even though they may have died, their prayers haven't, because though *we* live in time, God *doesn't*, and all those prayers those precious people prayed for me are even now pressing close to God, hands raised, saying, 'Me! Me!'"—a "metaphor moment."

The Table is one, too. Fred Craddock tells a story about preaching at a little church near Atlanta and being invited home to eat with this elderly woman. Her husband had died years before, and she had lived alone for more than twenty years in this big, rambling farm house. On the piano were old photographs of children and grandchildren and great-grandchildren. She said: "Now Dr. Craddock, you just sit here and read the paper or something. I'll have it ready in a few minutes."

He read the paper for a while and then decided to go into the kitchen to see if he could help. She wasn't in the kitchen, though; she was in the *dining room*—a big, formal dining room—setting this table that looked like it was an acre long! When he saw what she was doing, he said: "Uh, it's just my wife and me at home, so we eat in the kitchen at home." She never looked up. She took a tablecloth out of the credenza that had creases in it two inches thick! No telling how long it'd been since she'd used it. She spread it out on that table, and Craddock said: "Uh, we...we just...we just eat in the kitchen at home." She never said a word. She took some cloth napkins out of the credenza (you remember cloth napkins?) and put them in little Dresden China napkin rings with little roses on them and set two place settings at one end of the table across from each other. Craddock said: "You don't need to go to all this trouble. We eat in the kitchen at home." She opened the glass doors of the credenza and took out crystal stemware. Craddock said: "We eat in the kitchen." She said: "You want to go into the living room and read the paper?" He said: "That was gonna be my next suggestion. Why don't I go into the living room and read the paper."

About an hour later, she called him to dinner. It was a feast—roast beef, mashed potatoes and gravy, vegetables of every description, fresh baked bread, apple pie with ice cream for dessert.

During dinner, she looked at Craddock and said: "Dr. Craddock, do you know what it's like day after day to fix a meal for *one?*"

He said: "No ma'am."

She said: "Well, there's twice as many at this table today as have been here in months!"

Craddock and she gathered around that table and talked and laughed and ate. It was the Table! Would it be irreverent if I said that before that meal was over, it was the *Lord's* Table?

Shadows, echoes, dreams, odd moments in our lives that speak ambiguously and brokenly, but nonetheless powerfully, of that Presence.

Frederick Buechner tells a story about one of these "metaphor moments." He says that one spring in Vermont where he lives he was walking with a friend through a stand of maple trees at sugaring time. The sap buckets were hung from the trees, and if you were quiet, you could hear the sap dripping into them; all through the woods, if you kept still, you could hear the hushed drip-dropping of the sap into a thousand buckets or more hung out in the early spring woods with the sun coming down in long shafts of light through the trees. The sap of a maple is like rainwater, very soft and almost without taste except for the faintest tinge of sweetness to it, and when his friend said he'd never tasted it, Buechner offered to give him a taste. Buechner had to unhook the bucket from the tap to hold it for him, and when he bent his head down to drink from it, Buechner tipped the bucket down to his lips. Just as he was about to take a sip from the lifeblood of a tree, he looked up at Buechner and said, "You know, I have a feeling you ought to be saying some words or something."[1]

"In a little while you will see me no more, but if you look and if you listen, carefully...."

In one of the apocryphal gospels Jesus says: "Cleave the wood, and I am there; lift the stone, and I am there."

When I was doing post-doctoral work at Hebrew Union College and Jewish Institute of Religion in Cincinnati, I remember having a striking conversation with a rabbinical student one day over lunch. In a burst of impatience he said: "Don't you Christians get sick and tired of waiting for someone to come back who never comes back?" I said: "Is it *really* harder to wait for a Messiah who never comes back than it is to wait for a Messiah who never comes at all?" Though we'd been classmates, in that moment we became brothers.

Though he's gone, the fact that he was here will not let me go! Once in a while it happens—a piece of bread, a cup of wine, a prayer, a sip from a sweet bucket—and things flicker up out of our lives like a flame out of ashes we'd thought were long since dead. By flickering we see things that for a second or two make maybe not all the difference in the world, but enough of a difference to keep us at it.

"And now I am no more in the world, but *they* are in the world.... Holy Father, keep them in my name!"

We wait for him to come—more than we know, each of us waits for our heart's desire—and he comes in the "metaphor moments," in shadowy glimpses through tall and bleeding trees, at table, a *large* table for two, in long silences through which it seems some words should be spoken...or prayed.

"In a little while you will see me no more, but if you look, and if you listen, carefully...."

CHAPTER THREE

Glimpses of Glory

Luke 9:28-36

Did you see the movie *Stargate*? It's a wonderful movie, especially if, like me, you're fascinated with quantum mechanics and time travel. Actually, the premise of the story comes right off the front pages of the latest archaeological journals, if you read that kind of stuff. [I confess I do, though I'm not proud of it. I tried to give it up when I left the seminary, but alas it keeps beckoning me like the sirens of Odysseus. Now I'm trying to "taper off" slowly by reading *Biblical Archaeological Review*.]

In any case, there was a recent story about the three pyramids of Giza. These pyramids have puzzled archaeologists for years, for two reasons chiefly. The first is that the three pyramids are not of equal size. The first two are virtually identical while the third is significantly smaller. The second reason is that the third, smaller pyramid is also out of alignment with the other two. The three appear to have been constructed to be in line with each other, but the third, small pyramid is significantly off-set from the other two.

Finally, in exasperation, two astronomers were called in to consult on the matter. When they looked at the three pyramids, immediately they asked: "Do you have any aerial photographs of the pyramids?" Puzzled, the archaeologists said: "Sure, but why would you want *aerial* photographs?" They said: "Just a hunch." When the astronomers saw the aerial photos, instantly they said: "There it is!" The archaeologists said: "There *what* is?" The astronomers said: "Orion, of course!" When the archaeologists looked at the aerial photographs of the three pyramids,

29

they formed a perfect outline of Orion's belt—the two large pyramids obviously mimicking the two bright stars of Orion's belt, and the small pyramid, slightly offset from the other two, mimicking the smaller, third star of Orion's belt, slightly offset from the two brighter stars.

Well, the movie *Stargate* extended that premise to suggest that visitors from another world had instructed the ancient Egyptians in building the pyramids to be "extraterrestrial road signs" of a sort to guide them in their journeys to and from earth. [Incidentally, it is widely recognized that the pyramids were not only tombs for the pharaohs, but were also "launching pads" of sorts for them on their "other worldly journeys."] During some excavations at Giza, so the movie suggests, a portal was discovered with some hieroglyphs inscribed upon it which, when deciphered, transformed the portal into a "stargate" through which one could actually pass into another world!

Now if that sounds vaguely familiar to you, it should. The idea that "there's more here than meets the eye" and that if we could just find the door, marvelous journeys into other worlds would unfold before us is a common theme of a great deal of literature. It is, of course, the premise of Lewis Carrol's *Through the Looking Glass,* and C. S. Lewis's *The Chronicles of Narnia,* just to name two.

It is also the theme of one of the most curious and fascinating stories in the entire New Testament, the Transfiguration of Jesus. In Luke's version of the story, the Transfiguration is a direct response to two questions regarding Jesus' identity.

The first question is put by Herod Antipas upon hearing that Jesus had taken up, as it were, the preaching gauntlet of John the Baptist. Fearing that Jesus was somehow John come back to haunt him, Herod says: "John I beheaded; but who is this about whom I hear such things?" The second question regarding Jesus' identity is put by Jesus himself to his disciples: "But who do you say that I am?" When Simon Peter answers for the group, "You are God's Messiah," Jesus responds by predicting that as Messiah he will be rejected by his people, "suffer many things," and finally be put to death on the cross. Then, as though he had been listening in on the conversation, God offers his own answer to the question of Jesus' identity in the form of an epiphany we call "The Transfiguration."

Though all three Synoptics describe the scene, Luke's version is distinctive, especially in its heavy use of Old Testament imagery. Notice, only Luke says that the Transfiguration happened "as they were praying," that is, seeking the presence [an audience?] of God. Suddenly, Luke says, Jesus' face, and clothes curiously enough, were altered, becoming "dazzling white" with glory. Moses and Elijah (the Law and the Prophets) appeared, Luke says, "in glory" talking with Jesus, and only Luke among the Synoptics tells us what they were talking about— his *exodus*. Not his "departure" as the RSV has it, but *exodus*, an explicit allusion to the OLD TESTAMENT Exodus in which Israel was set free from Egyptian slavery, and an oblique reference to Jesus' impending death which will set the new People of God free from a slavery of a different kind. Only Luke tells us that the disciples were "heavy with sleep" as peering into a "dream world." Did they really see it, or was it all a dream?

Luke says a "cloud overshadowed them; and they were afraid as they entered it." As you know, the cloud is the standard Old Testament image for the *Shekinah Yhwh*, the "glory" of God. One could not actually see God, only his "aura" as it were, his *Shekinah*, his "glory," hence the disciples' fear. Luke is deliberately casting his story in the imagery of the Exodus, and specifically Moses' encounter with the *Shekinah Yhwh* on Horeb's heights, an encounter, you will recall, that left Moses' face shining with the residue of "Glory." Like Moses before him, Jesus ascends the mountain and passes through to the "other side," permitting the bleary-eyed disciples to "glimpse the glory," even though momentarily, of Jesus' true identity. It's an epiphany, a "breakthrough," a "metaphor moment" as I've called it elsewhere, of the blinding, radiant Presence and Glory of God.

What does it all mean, these "glimpses of glory," these epiphanies of the presence of God in our lives? Once again, C. S. Lewis has helped us here. In what is, I believe, the finest book ever written on *Miracles*, Lewis argues compellingly that biblical miracles are of two types— "miracles of the old creation" and "miracles of the new creation." "Miracles of the old creation" are those events in which God does close and small, suddenly and locally, what he does everyday through the whole process of the natural order, but on a scale so grand that no one much notices.

For example, when Jesus heals a leper, he's not violating the laws of nature, he's focusing them, concentrating them, localizing them. All healing is, in the final analysis, *divine* healing. The physician's role is but to accelerate the body's own natural [God-given, I would add] healing processes, or to remove that which inhibits health and wholeness;

but no physician, strictly speaking, *heals* anyone. No one who doesn't *want* to be healed is ever healed, without their knowledge or consent. Did you ever hear of a doctor healing a cut on a corpse?

"Miracles of the new creation," Lewis says, are those epiphanies, those "metaphor moments" when a New Nature "breaks through," revealing itself. Another world, Transcendence itself, is pulled like a blanket over ordinary time and ordinary history and then, from time to time, "spikes down" through it, revealing itself and thereby transforming the ordinary into the extraordinary.

If that sounds a little far-fetched, a little too much "smoke and mirrors" for you, listen to Lewis describe it:

> It is useful to remember that even now senses responsive to different vibrations would admit us to quite new worlds of experience: that a multi-dimensional space would be different, almost beyond recognition, from the space we are now aware of, yet not discontinuous from it: that time may not always be for us, as it now is, unilinear and irreversible: that other parts of Nature might some day obey us as our own cerebral cortex now does. It is useful not because we can trust these fancies to give us any positive truths about the New Creation but because they teach us not to limit, in our rashness, the vigour and variety of the new crops which this old field might yet produce.[1]

The Transfiguration is a miracle of the *new creation,* a "glimpse of glory" that reminds us that there's more here than meets the eye, that the prosaic and the pedestrian are not the whole story, that every now and then "holiness" shines through the "humanness" and we see it all clearly if not fully.

Every now and again it happens that way, and we "glimpse the glory," and those glimpses, though fragmentary and ephemeral, can make all the difference.

It made the difference for Simon. It was the summer of 64, that's A.D. 64, when Simon, according to a late second-century Christian writing known as *The Acts of Peter,* was slinking out of Rome incognito, fleeing Nero's program against the Christians there. It seems that one of them, Marcellus, had enjoined Peter to escape Nero's wrath by withdrawing to a safe place there to wait out the persecution, "for the good of the 'cause,'" Marcellus said. Simon protested: "Shall we act like deserters, brothers?" Marcellus said: "No, it is so that you can go on serving the Lord"; and so donning disguise, Peter left the city.

At the city's gate, he saw the risen Jesus entering Rome and asked him: "Where are you going, Lord?" (*Quo vadis, Domine?* in the Latin). Jesus answered: "I am going to Rome to be crucified again!" At that word, so the legend goes, Peter turned around and returned to the city, where he was captured and executed.

When he was brought to the place of his execution, he boldly told all who watched of Christ's appearance to him at the city gates, and how "glimpsing the glory" had stopped him in his tracks and sent him back. Then, with voice clear and strong, Peter announced to those assembled: "Simon, it is now time for you to surrender your body to those who are taking it."

Then, turning to his executioners, he said: "Take it, then, you whose duty this is. I request you, therefore, to crucify me head-downwards in this way and no other, for I am not worthy to be crucified in the same manner as was my Lord."

Heather Elkins "glimpsed the glory." She tells a story about being a volunteer chaplain at a maximum security prison during the Christmas season. She decided that they would do a "live nativity" to help the inmates "get into the spirit" of Christmas. Like God, she had to use what she had at hand, being permitted to take nothing into the prison. The frayed blankets were transfigured into realistic shepherds' cloaks. Sheets, a far cry from being radiantly white, draped "angels" and a smooth-shaven "Mary." There were some natural advantages to the setting, however. A prison yard needed no imagination to be transformed into the barren hills of Bethlehem. There were even "Roman" guards who kept watch over their "flocks" by day and night from the tower and the walls.

The only snag was the baby Jesus. What could they put in the cardboard box that masqueraded as a manger? A swaddling towel? A handmade doll? They wanted to *see* Jesus! Right there, at the end of the year, in a corner of a yard, in the presence of a "captive" audience, shall we say, a *transfiguration* happened. They saw Jesus as he is! As the scraggly shepherds came, wrapped in their ragged reputations; as the king knelt, crowned with aluminum; as the far-from-angelic chorus sang, "Mary" lifted the child for all to see, the only "Jesus" they knew, the only "Jesus" they had—a handmade *crucifix!* Gripped by the Glory, they sang the best Christmas carol of all, "Amazing Grace, how sweet the sound, that saved a wretch like me!"[2]

"And they spoke of his *exodus* which he was to accomplish in Jerusalem."

Sometimes it happens that way, and we "glimpse the glory," and suddenly we see it all clearly, if not fully—who he really is, and who we really are, and what, in Him, we can really be.

However, the cross comes before the crown, and tomorrow is a Monday morning. You can't get to Easter without going through Lent, because there can be no resurrection until somebody dies.

In the meantime, *on the way,* we'll remember those "glimpses of glory" and we'll follow the "Shining Face."

CHAPTER FOUR

Epiphany

John 2:1-11

Something invariably goes wrong at weddings. Have you noticed that? The florist runs late, the tuxedos don't fit, the in-laws get angry, your best friends don't show up, but your crazy Uncle George does. It's not really surprising that weddings are such magnets for mishap when you consider what they really are—high church and state occasions involving amateurs under pressure. I guess it's because of sheer grace that most of them turn out as well as they do!

I've done several hundred weddings since being ordained back in 1972, and I thought I'd seen it all, but the wedding story Robert Fulghum tells in his book *It Was On Fire When I Lay Down On It* takes the "wedding cake." I warn you, those of you out there who are planning your own weddings or the weddings of your children may not want to listen to this.

The central figure in this wedding debacle was the mother of the bride, MOTB for short. This normally sane and intelligent woman went through an amazing transformation at the announcement of her daughter's engagement—she became unhinged. Nobody knew it, but she had been quietly waiting for this day with a script for a production that would make Cecil B. Demille look like a rank amateur. In the seven months prior to the wedding day, she checked and rechecked every possible detail of the wedding, leaving nothing to chance or human error. Everything that could be engraved was engraved. The minister met with the bride and groom three times during that seven month period; the MOTB he met with weekly! His secretary announced her visits simply by saying: "She's here." No further introduction was needed.

Well, the big day finally, and I do mean finally, arrived. Guests in formal attire packed the church. Enough candles were lit to render a fire marshall catatonic. Then, in all her regal splendor, the MOTB coasted down the aisle to take her seat of honor, there to view the spectacle she'd been orchestrating for seven months.

Unbeknownst to her, however, the bride was sequestered in the church reception hall with her father there to await the big moment. She'd been dressed for hours, if not days. By this time, she was so nervous that she wasn't even sure who it was she was marrying anymore. No adrenaline was left in her body. Nervously, she began to walk along the tables laden with gourmet goodies and absentmindedly sampled the little pink, yellow, and green mints. Then she picked through the silver bowls of mixed nuts, followed by a cheese ball or two, some black olives, a handful of glazed almonds, a little sausage with a frilly toothpick stuck in it, a couple of shrimp blanketed in bacon, and a cracker piled with liver paté. To wash it all down—a glass of pink champagne which her father gave to her to calm her nerves.

When she finally arrived at the door of the church for the wedding march, what you noticed first was not her dress, but her face—it had this sickly green cast to it. What was coming down the aisle was not a bride, but a walking grenade with the pin pulled out.

Then it happened. Just as she walked past her mother, the bride threw up, and I mean "threw up." This was no polite ladylike indiscretion into some hanky; she hosed the chancel! She wasted the bridesmaids, the groom, the ring bearer, and the minister! Having disgorged her hors d'oeuvres, champagne, and the last of her dignity, the bride went limp in her father's arms while the MOTB fainted dead away. Later, when the chaos had subsided and the bride revived, it was decided that the wedding would go on. Cecil would have wanted it that way. As the ceremony finally got cranked up again, only two people were seen to be smiling—the mother of the groom and the father of the bride![1]

Don't you love weddings? All kinds of things can go wrong at weddings.

That's nothing new. In our gospel lesson John tells us about a near disaster at a wedding in Cana of Galilee. If you think weddings can be big events in our world, you should have seen the way weddings were conducted in the ancient oriental world of first-century Judaism.

Marriage in first-century Judaism actually began with betrothal (*kiddushin*) which was legally binding on the couple, the betrothal ceremony culminating in the writing of a marriage contract or *ketubah* which stipulated how the bride was acquired and when the marriage proper would occur. You will remember that Joseph, upon learning that Mary was pregnant, contemplated divorcing her—strange to us in that they were only engaged. Among first-century Jews, the *kiddushin* was as binding as actual marriage.

The marriage ceremony itself took place amidst great pomp and ceremony, usually about a year after the signing of the *ketubah*. It most often took place on a Tuesday, the "third day." You see, it was believed that Tuesday, the "third day," was a particularly blessed day for a wedding, because in the creation story in Genesis Tuesday was the only day which was twice "blessed," and so any wedding occurring on Tuesday, the "third day," was also "twice blessed" (note that John says that this wedding occurred "on the third day").

I was in Israel some time ago with some folk from my church, and we walked over to the King David Hotel one evening about dusk just to look around. It's a very famous hotel in old Jerusalem in which kings and presidents and dignitaries usually stay while in the Holy City. When we walked into the lobby, we noticed that a large crowd had gathered on the patio there overlooking the Old City. When we investigated further, it was a wedding! With the sun going down on a breath-taking view of Jerusalem, the rabbi was leading the couple through a reading from the Torah as they declared their love for each other in God's presence; and yes, it was Tuesday, the "third day."

On the great day a tent (*chapheh*) would be spread, under which the wedding ceremony was conducted. That practice is preserved today in the bridal canopy used in Jewish weddings. The canopy symbolized the "canopy of the heavens" spread out above the couple as a sign that God was present to "witness" their marriage and thus to bless it. Today the canopy is usually sky blue to reflect the idea of the "canopy of the heavens," the *ha shamayim* of Genesis 1. All around the blessed occasion, both before and after the ceremony itself, was the party, the feast that the guests would enjoy with singing and dancing and eating and drinking, often continuing for the entire week!

That's why when Mary came to Jesus with the revelation: "Son, we're out of wine!" the tension became palpable. You see, in an oriental culture hospitality is the most prized virtue. To run out of wine at a wedding party was a faux pas every bit as big as the one Fulghum describes in his story, because the hosts would have thereby "lost face" with their guests, an unthinkable shame in the oriental world.

Mary and Jesus have words: "Son, can't you do something?" Jesus responds: "Woman, what have you to do with me? My hour has not yet come." Mary, being the good Jewish mother, did what good Jewish mothers do, and after a while Jesus acquiesced. He tells the servants to fill the six stone water jars, kept for Jewish purification rites, to the brim. Each one held about 20 or 30 gallons of water. I told you it was a big wedding! Quick as a flash, Jesus had turned the water into wine. When the maitre d' tasted the wine he exclaimed: "Boy! This is good stuff! I'm impressed. Hosts usually serve the good stuff first, and then when everyone has had a little too much, they bring out the watered down stuff so no one will notice, but you've saved the best for last!" John adds the epilogue: "Now this was the first of Jesus' signs."

Did you get that? John called it a "sign," *semeia* in the Greek. That's John's word for the miracles—"signs." That is, there's more here than meets the eye. It's his way of saying: "Don't get so hung up on the miracle that you fail to see the real miracle here. Don't focus so much on what happened that you fail to see what really happened." He calls them "signs," breakthroughs, epiphanies in which the everyday is transformed by the eternal, the prosaic by the poetic.

This story is an "epiphany story" in which the glory of God breaks through and transforms those who see it—"and the disciples believed in him."

John makes that clear to us in two ways—one explicit, one subtle. In a direct statement John says: "This, the first of his signs, Jesus did at Cana in Galilee, and manifested his glory." If you're reading the story carefully, you already know that this story is about more than a wine shortage. Remember, John began by telling us that the marriage happened "on the third day." As I said, Tuesday was, and is, the favorite day for Jewish weddings, but "the third day" is also a resurrection symbol, the day when new life "broke out" and "broke through."

It's John's way of saying: "This is no ordinary wedding; it's an epiphany of the grace of God, a "window onto another world" revealing to us a miraculous, new life that "breaks through" and takes us completely by surprise.

Sometimes it happens that way, these "epiphanies" of the grace of God.

Isak Dinesen in her wonderful short story called *Babette's Feast* tells about one of these epiphanies. Babette is a French refugee down on her luck who is taken in by a small Scandinavian religious sect. They are a strict and pious, gentle and joyless people, rejecting any hint of worldliness. Babette works for them, cooking and sharing in their somber meal-times. When Babette receives a financial legacy, however, she shows her gratitude to her Christian friends by preparing a wonderful feast for them—it turns out she was one of Paris' renowned chefs. In that feast prepared in love, those austere believers discover the grace of God in a way they had never before known. What had begun a supper had ended a sacrament.[2]

Ferrol Sams, a fiction writer and medical doctor from Fayetteville, Georgia, has written a wonderful collection of short stories called *Epiphany*. The title story is about a family doctor of the old school, Dr. Mark Goddard, who has become frustrated and disillusioned with the high-tech, low-touch approach to medicine that's invaded the clinic where he practices. The clinic has brought in a young Turkish adminis-trator named Dennis who officiously rides herd on the physicians to make sure that they (1) see as many patients as possible, taking up as little time as possible with each, and (2) practice their medicine not so much with a view toward helping their patients as to avoiding litigation and liability. Dr. Goddard not only detests this assembly-line approach to medicine, but he chafes at Dennis's obtrusive and bureaucratic style. He constantly rails against what he calls the "new trinity" in medicine of "Medicare, Malpractice, and Medical Records."

To "get Dennis's goat," Dr. Goddard, who loves poetry, regularly inter-sperses lines from A. E. Housman and Edna St. Vincent Millay and Lewis Carroll and Robert Browning throughout his "patient encounter logs" when he dictates them, knowing that the transcriptionists will notify the clinic administrator's office of this grievous breach of medical procedure, which will then send Dennis flying into Dr. Goddard's office protesting: "How would this look in a courtroom should your logs ever be subpoe-naed, quoting poetry in a patient log like that!" Ole Doc Goddard responds that should Dennis stop just long enough to lift his nose out of his spreadsheets and deposit it in some of that poetry he's always railing about, he might just learn that there's more going on around him than bottom lines and patient logs.

That's about the only diversion in Dr. Goddard's otherwise drab and pedestrian life, until a new patient comes to see him— Gregry McHune—that's "Gregry" with no "O." Ostensibly, he comes in to have his high blood pressure treated, but as he returns week after week, a strange friendship develops. In many ways, they have absolutely nothing in com-mon—Dr. Goddard is a highly educated, extremely literate Renaissance man trapped in a system that doesn't understand him and for which he has no respect, and Gregry is a rough, red-necked, blue-collar, six-packing "good ole boy" who's done time in the state prison for manslaughter. As the weeks go by, Dr. Goddard spends less and less time treating Gregry and more and more time listening to him. As he learns more and more of Gregry's story, he discovers in Gregry a human spirit struggling heroically against incredible odds to "do the right thing," and he's drawn to him like a moth to a flame.

Then a strange thing begins to happen. Goddard discovers that in this bizarre friendship with this man who seemed to have nothing at all to offer him, he is, in fact, receiving more than he's giving. He rediscovers, in the simple relationship that the brief encounters between doctor and patient affords, a renaissance, a rebirth, an epiphany, if you will, of his own life and vitality and purpose. He says to Gregry after one session in which Gregry had held him spell-bound, telling him of his hard and cruel life: "Gregry McHune, you are an epiphany! I am constantly amazed at the resilience of the human spirit and humbled by the manifestation of unanticipated grace."[3]

John says that day in Cana was the first of Jesus' signs. It was a biggy— turning water into wine! The disciples must have been pleased that they had chosen so well, following such a high-powered Messiah. They didn't know—how could they know—where He would ultimately take them, that things would get complicated and confused, that one day they would drink wine together one last time and Jesus would talk not of water and weddings, but of body and blood—his and theirs—and the joy and jubilation of Cana would seem a faint and distant memory.

You don't know what lies ahead for you either. When you leave this Sunday celebration, there will be less glorious moments on your journey. One hour of joy doesn't nullify the late night phone call, or the early morning diagnosis, or the end of the week pink slip. When you leave this sanctuary, you must go back into an always pedestrian, sometimes dangerous world where hope is in short supply.

As you go, remember the epiphanies—the breakthroughs, those grace-filled moments when the "real" pierced the "sham" and you saw it all clearly, if not fully—moments in which right in the middle of the everyday Eternity happened, and the water became wine, and supper became sacrament, and friendship became communion.

When the darkness returns—and it will, it will—hold on to that God who saves the best for last, and who saves the last one best. Please!

PART TWO

THE SOUGHT

CHAPTER FIVE

The Hound of Heaven

Psalm 23

Today we're visiting with an old friend, you and I—the Twenty-Third Psalm. It was the very first passage of scripture I ever memorized. Was it yours? When I conduct a funeral and I ask the family what was their loved one's favorite passage of scripture, the answer always is, *always*, the Twenty-Third Psalm.

If I were to ask you today, "What is God like? With what picture do you imagine Him?" before the question has taken solid shape, the words are already forming in your mind: "The LORD is my shepherd, I shall not want." There are many metaphors and similes that the scripture employs in its attempt to "capture" something of the nature of God, but surely this is our favorite: "God is like a shepherd who protects and cares for his sheep." Indeed, so deep is the image, so pervasive the metaphor, that only in one place in the New Testament does a literal reference to shepherds even occur—Luke 2, "And there were shepherds tending their flocks by night." Everywhere else, *everywhere*, when the word "shepherd" occurs, the reference is either to God or Jesus!

I have to admit, however, that this particular simile loses some of its appeal when you realize that if God is the "Shepherd," that makes you and me the sheep. Think about it. What are sheep known for? Well, they're dumb, dirty, smelly, destructive, and absolutely helpless. I don't know about you, but I don't know if I like that! What's worse, look around! You have to say, that picture of the human race is closer to the mark than we'd like to admit!

All of that notwithstanding, the sense of reassurance I get is undiminished when I hear the words, "The Lord is my shepherd."

43

Everytime I see sheep, *everytime*, I think about those words. Do you?

When I turned to our sermon lesson for today, I knew I'd come home—Psalm 23, our old friend, the Shepherd Psalm. When you read it, it's kinda like going home after you've been away for a while.

Some years ago, my dad and I went back to Belle Glade, Florida, a town on the south end of Lake Okeechobee, where my dad had worked for many years. Dad was a vice president with a large agribusiness, and the towns around the lake were small, so everybody knew him. He'd been retired and living on the coast for ten years. I mean, life goes on! Dad's company had changed in the interim. One generation passes the torch to another and all that.

Well, Dad and I walked into the local Red Wing Feed and Supply Store to buy some sunflower seeds for his squirrels. Dad fed the squirrels every morning at 5:30—every morning! I mean, the squirrels count on him! You can understand that, can't you?

Well, there was this young man behind the counter who took our order and loaded the 100-pound bag of sunflower seeds in the trunk of Dad's car. He'd been retired for ten years, and he hadn't been in that store for twenty, but when Dad reached for his wallet to pay him, this kid whom neither of us had ever met before so far as we knew looked at my father and said: "You want me to put that on your ticket, Mr. Stacy?" Now, for those of you who've lived in the city all your life, "ticket" in those days was a small town euphemism for an open account by which merchants would supply local folk with credit. The townspeople, then, would come by, usually once a month or so, to "square up." Though Dad hadn't been in that store in years, this kid asked him: "You want me to just put that on your ticket, Mr. Stacy?"

My work has taken me all over this country. I've moved about a lot, and to be honest, "home" was wherever I "hung my hat," so to speak, but that experience made me aware of something I'd missed through the years more than I had realized—"home," home—someplace I know and someplace I am known. My father, who worked for the same company for 43 years, had such a place, and no matter how long he'd been away, when he returned, he was home.

"You want me to put that on your ticket?"

"Home"—that's something of the feeling I get when I read Psalm 23. "The Lord is my shepherd, I shall not want."

You know, I can't even remember when I didn't know this Psalm. Can you? I've run across people who've never memorized a verse of scripture who know this Psalm. Did you see it when you came to worship this morning here at First Baptist Shelby? Out in the narthex, watching over you like a "Tiffany tower in time of trouble"—Christ the Good Shepherd.

"He makes me lie down in green pastures. He leads me beside still waters. He restores my soul." Sheep don't drink from dangerous, swift-flowing wadis or streams. They could fall in and drown, you know. "He leads me beside still waters." This Shepherd takes care of His sheep.

The metaphor continues: "Though I walk through the valley of the shadow of death." That word, "valley," in Hebrew, "gaye," really means "wadi," those low-lying places all over Palestine which, though they may be dry as dust one moment, can fill up with rainfall and become a sudden torrent, washing away everything in their path—a fitting metaphor to describe the inundating abyss of death. Do you get it? The Shepherd leads the sheep to quiet, still waters, but when they must face the raging torrent that is death, the Shepherd is there too, guarding, protecting, preserving his sheep: "I will fear no evil, for you are with me."

Did I tell you that the most requested passage at funerals is this old friend—the Shepherd Psalm? Part of the reason that is so, I am sure, is that when life runs out into deep water, we invariably look for something familiar, commonplace, to reassure us that some things don't change; some things remain unaffected by the chaos.

A woman comes home from the cemetery just having buried her husband of forty years and starts washing the dishes—you know, the ones with the tape on the bottom to tell you whose they are.

"Mom, don't do that now. The girls and I'll do that later. Come sit down with us and rest."

"Honestly, I don't know what to do with her; washing dishes at a time like this."

A few minutes later, as the conversation at the table lulls, she's back at the sink again.

"Mom, don't do that now!"

Leave her alone! Let her wash the dishes. In the chaos, she has to know that some things stay the same!

Isn't part of the reason we turn to this Psalm because it dares to speak boldly about death, that dark valley, and calls it, too, a place where the Shepherd leads? When life makes us feel as though God has a lot of explaining to do, here comes our old friend, Psalm 23, gently reminding us of "green pastures" and "still waters," and a God Who is, after all, like a Shepherd, leading us, restoring us, protecting us, comforting us.

I was so relieved in doing my sermon preparation this week to find my old friend Psalm 23. I had a great sermon going, too, until, that is, I turned the page. You see, in my Hebrew text, verse 6 is on the next page, and so, I turned the page and there it was: "Surely goodness and mercy shall follow me all the days of my life." You see, here's a good reason never to prepare your sermons from the original languages; it can ruin a good sermon! I was doing just fine until I read verse 6 in Hebrew. I even had a cute little story to tell. Want to hear it?

At the famous castle high on the hill in Heidelberg, Germany, over the arched entrance to the castle they're there, watching over you—twin angels carved in the stone portal. Most people don't see them, never look up; but they're there: Goodness and Mercy, following you with their eyes.

A little girl was listening as the tour guide told about the two angels over the portal, and she asked: "But where's the third one?"

"Third one? What do you mean, third one?"

"Shirley. Where's Shirley? You know, like the Bible says: Shirley, Goodness, and Mercy shall follow me...."

I mean, I was on a roll! "I'll knock this sermon out in an hour."

You can imagine, then, my embarrassment when I discovered that the Hebrew text didn't say what I thought it said at all. I was all ready for "Goodness and Mercy" to "follow me all the days of my life." I already had images running though my mind of ole "Shep the Sheep Dog," gently rounding up strays, herding them with well-chosen barks and playful little nips toward the pasture where they could rest and graze. When I read the Hebrew I panicked, closed my Masoretic text, and looked around to see if anybody noticed. It doesn't say what I thought it said: "Goodness and Mercy shall follow me all the days of my life;" it says: "Goodness and Mercy shall hound me all the days of my life!" That's right. I looked it up. The word in the Hebrew is *yirdephuni*, from the Hebrew root word *radaph*, which means "to pursue." Remember when the Pharaoh's chariots pursued the children of Israel to the sea? *Radaph*!

In another Psalm, also attributed to David, the Shepherd King sings "I pursued my enemies and overtook them; I did not turn back until they were consumed." You want to guess what the Hebrew word is that's translated "pursued?" *Radaph*.

"Surely Goodness and Mercy shall pursue me all the days of my life." This is no "Shep the Sheep Dog;" this is the Hound of Heaven!"

Professor Elmo Scoggin, a member of First Baptist Church of Raleigh where I was pastor and an expert in Biblical Hebrew, tells me that the inspiration for this imagery comes from a type of hound that used to be indigenous to Palestine called a saluki, a dog that was most noted for its ability to sniff out a trail even as old as eight days! You put this hound on the trail, and he never gives up. The Psalmist says: "Surely Goodness and

Mercy shall hound me all the days of my life!" Get it? Kind of puts a little different slant on things, doesn't it?

Here I am, bumping along through life, half asleep, thinking only of God when it's convenient to do so. Suddenly, there over my shoulder come Goodness and Mercy loping along after me.

"Hmm. Aren't Goodness and Mercy coming up behind me kinda' fast?"

"Huh, can you beat that? Boy they're really moving! Look at 'em run!"

"You know, now that I look at 'em, are they following me or are they chasing me? It's hard to tell."

"Oh my, they're not following; they're chasing, they're pursuing me, hounding me!"

In his classic old poem *The Hound of Heaven*, Francis Thompson caught it way back in 1913.

> *I fled Him, down the night and down the days;*
> *I fled him, down the arches of the years;*
> *I fled Him, down the labyrinthine ways*
> *   Of my own mind; and in the mist of tears*
> *I hid from Him...*
> *   From those strong Feet that followed, followed after.*[1]

Do you still think you know this Shepherd?

C. S. Lewis knew him. In his autobiography titled *Surprised By Joy*, he wrote of his own experience of being "hounded" by the Grace of God. He was an atheist, by his own admission, teaching philosophy at Oxford when he encountered "Goodness" and her sister "Mercy." He wrote:

> You must picture me alone in that room in Magdalen, night after night, feeling, whenever my mind lifted even for a second from my work, the steady, unrelenting approach of Him whom I so earnestly desired not to meet. That which I greatly feared had at last come upon me. In the Trinity Term of 1929 I gave in, and admitted that God was God, and knelt and prayed: perhaps, that night, the most dejected and reluctant convert in all England. I did not then see what is now the most shining and obvious thing; the Divine humility which will accept a convert even on such terms. The Prodigal Son at least walked home on his own feet. But who can duly adore that Love which will open the high gates to a prodigal who is brought in kicking, struggling, resentful, and darting his eyes in every direction for a

chance of escape? The words *compelle intrare*, compel them to come in, have been so abused by wicked men that we shudder at them; but, properly understood, they plumb the depth of the Divine Mercy. The hardness of God is kinder than the softness of men, and His compulsion is our liberation.[2]

"Surely, Goodness and Mercy shall hound me all the days of my life!"

Duke Chapel's Will Willimon tells a story about an old, crusty, bitter man he once knew. Some said his bitterness was justified. His beloved wife died giving birth to their only child. The child died shortly thereafter due to birth complications.

"I'm sorry; we did everything we could," they said.

He never went to church, never had anything to do with anyone. When, in his late sixties, they carried him out of his small, dark apartment to the hospital room to die, no one visited, no flowers were delivered, no cards sent. They asked him: "Do you want a telephone in your room?" He said: "What for? No one's gonna call."

There was this nurse. I think her name was "Mercy." Or was it "Goodness?" I forget. Well, she wasn't actually a nurse yet, just a student nurse, a "nurse-in-training," and because she was in training she didn't know everything that they teach you in school about not getting too close to your patients—you know, the need for detachment, objectivity, and all that. She kinda liked the old man, in spite of the fact that he was rude to her, told her to "Go away and bother someone else."

She just smiled and tried to coax him to eat his Jello. At night, she'd tuck him in and ask: "Do you need anything? Is there anything I can get for you?"

"No. Leave me alone! Don't need anybody to help me," he'd growl at her.

Soon, his ole bark turned into a whimper—too weak to resist. Late at night, after her regular duties, she'd pull up a chair, sit by the bed, and sing to him as she stroked his old, gnarled hand. He looked up at her in the dim light of the hospital room and wondered to himself if he saw in that face the face of a little one he'd never gotten to see grow up. A tear formed in the corner of his eye when she leaned over and kissed him good night on his wrinkled old forehead.

She leaned down over the bed to kiss him, and as she did, she whispered in his ear the last word that hard, old crusty codger ever heard before he slipped out into the dark valley of the shadow of death. She said: "Gotcha!"[3]

God on the Gallows

Luke 23:26-49

There is a story that haunts me in the night. I read it years ago, but it haunts me still. It haunts me in part because I know it's true. It happened; it really happened. It haunts me in part because of the skill of the storyteller; the economy with which the story is told cuts like a scalpel. Most of all, it's the question that haunts me, that awful question I cannot get out of my mind.

The story is told in a little book by Elie Wiesel simply titled *Night*. Wiesel is a survivor of the Holocaust and a Pulitzer prize-winning professor at Boston University (although he says no one who was there ever *really* survived the Holocaust). Following his nightmare at Auschwitz in which as a teenager he lost everyone he ever loved, Wiesel vowed he would not speak or write of his experiences at Auschwitz and Büchenwald until twenty years had passed, lest he profane them by his lack of perspective. *Night* was the book with which he broke the silence. It's a hundred pages of gut-wrenching memories in the "night," and among them this one:

In the story, Wiesel tells of his experience of witnessing a hanging at Buna, one of the concentration camps where he was interned during the war. An electric power station was blown up, and the Gestapo suspected sabotage. They rounded up the most likely suspects for interrogation, among them a Dutchman, the Oberkapo of the camp, a prisoner who had been placed over his fellow prisoners in order to maintain order among the ranks. The Oberkapo was tortured in a vain attempt to get him to reveal the identities of those involved in the

49

plot. He was transferred to Auschwitz and never heard from again, but his little assistant, a young boy known in the camp as a "pipel," was retained also for interrogation. He too was tortured in an attempt to secure the identities of his co-conspirators. He too was silent; and so the Gestapo sentenced him to be hanged along with two others who had been discovered hiding a cache of arms.

One afternoon following work, Wiesel and the others returned to the spectre of three gallows in the camp courtyard. The prisoners were ordered to watch while the head of the camp read the verdict. The three victims were then mounted onto chairs with their necks in nooses. The two adults, in a futile gesture of defiance, shouted "Long live liberty!" The little boy was silent.

Finally, at a sign from the head of the camp, the three chairs were tipped over. Then the prisoners were forced to file past to watch the three die as a deterrent to further insurrection. Wiesel says that the two adults died almost immediately, their tongues swollen and blue. The boy, being much lighter than they, was still alive. For more than a half-hour, Wiesel says, he hung there struggling between life and death. Each member of the camp had to file past and look him in the face as he died. Wiesel writes:

> Behind me, I heard [a] man asking:
> "Where is God now?"
> And I heard a voice within me answer him:
> "Where is He? Here He is—He is hanging here on the
>   gallows...."
> That night the soup tasted of corpses.[2]

Now you're haunted too. I trust you realize that this is not the first time the question, "Where is God?" has been asked. Luke in his version of the crucifixion of Jesus plays out this scene with chilling similarity. He even describes the scene as a "hanging," *kremasthenton*. While Matthew and Mark both remark that the two who were executed with Jesus "reviled him," Luke alone tells us what they said.

"Are you not the Christ?" one of them asked. "Then save yourself and us!" You could translate it: "Where is your God now?"

"But the other rebuked him, saying, 'Do you not fear God, for you are in the same judgment. And we appropriately so, but this man has done nothing wrong.'"

He asks the age-old question: Why would God let an innocent man suffer? How can God stand by idly and watch this happen? It is not so much Jesus who is on trial here as God! "Where is God?" he asked. "Where is He?"

Then, as though somewhere in his pain and agony a tumbler clicks in, he sees it. God isn't *watching* this innocent man hang on the gallows; God is *on* the gallows! Turning to Jesus he says: "Jesus, remember me when you come to your kingdom," not "when your kingdom *comes,*" but "when you come to your kingdom."

Jesus says: "Today you will be with me in Paradise."

This is a very, very different picture of the meaning of the death of Christ than the one to which we're accustomed. We do the same thing to the death of Christ that we do to the birth of Christ—we run all the accounts together into a single story, conflating some events, dismissing others. When Luke is read *vertically*, without looking over our shoulders at Mark or Paul or Hebrews, we're able to see just how unique his interpretation of the death of Christ really is.

For example, unlike the interpretation of the death of Jesus in Mark's gospel or in the letters of Paul or particularly in the Epistle to the Hebrews, Luke carefully avoids any connection between Jesus' death and the forgiveness of sins. This is sometimes called "the doctrine of the atonement" or "expiation theology," from the Latin *expiare,* literally, "to get the sin out." In this view, Jesus' death is seen as somehow "atoning" for our sins, setting right what has gone wrong, "balancing the cosmic scales," or "satisfying God's sense of justice."

In Mark, when James and John are arguing over who will be greater in the Kingdom, Jesus will say: "The Son of Man came not to be served but to serve and to give his life a ransom (*luvtron*) for many." Luke, however, moves this whole discussion to the table—rather ironic don't you think—and avoids any mention of an atoning death: "I am among you as one who serves." In Romans 3:25, when Paul describes the "redemption which is in Christ Jesus," he says, "God put [him] forward to be an *expiation*" (*hilasterion*, a sacrificial term) for our sins. The writer of Hebrews, who interprets Jesus' death exclusively in terms of the Day of Atonement ritual, says it plainly: "Without the shedding of blood there is no remission of sins."

Not Luke—Luke carefully avoids any relationship between the Cross and forgiveness of sins. It's not that he doesn't believe Jesus can forgive sins; on the contrary, in Luke's gospel Jesus is forever running around forgiving sins; only he does it long before he gets to Golgotha. He forgives the sins of the paralytic in chapter five. In chapter seven Jesus forgives the sins of a "woman of the city," Luke calls her, who washed Jesus' feet with her tears and dried them with her hair. "Therefore I tell you," says Jesus, "her sins, which are many, are forgiven." In chapter nineteen Jesus forgives the sins of the tax collector Zacchaeus and says to him: "Today salvation has come to this house." Following the resurrection, the Risen Lord tells his confused, bewildered disciples that it was all right there in the Scriptures if they had only read them: "Thus it is written, that the Christ should suffer, and on the third day rise from the dead, and that repentance and forgiveness of sins should be preached in his name to all nations."

Luke clearly believes Jesus can forgive sins; but the difference is this: in Luke Jesus forgives sins *before* the Cross and *after* the Cross, but not *at* the Cross. Because for Luke, the Cross is not an *expiation* of sins, it's an *epiphany* of the love of God, God's supreme act of love shining through, overcoming our ignorance and blindness. Only in Luke does Jesus pray from the cross, "Father forgive them, they don't know what they're doing." Notice, Jesus isn't forgiving sins here; he's asking *God* to. In Luke, the effect of the Cross is less "cosmic" and more "personal," less "legal" and more "relational." It's not so much "well, now that that's out of the way, maybe we can be friends again," as it is "I never *knew* you cared that much!"

If I were to ask you to describe a tree to me, you might say, "Well, it has bark and leaves and branches and roots." If I took an axe to the tree and cut it down, you'd say, "Oh, I see now! It has rings too!" It's not that the rings didn't exist until I cut the tree down; it's that you just couldn't see them quite so clearly until I cut the tree down.

That's Luke's theology. God has always been like the God we see in Jesus of Nazareth. It's just that on the Cross we see His heart in a way we've never seen it before. In Mark, Jesus cries: "My God, my God, why have you abandoned me?" God doesn't abandon Jesus in Luke's story. Instead Luke lets the criminal ask our question for us. "Where is your God now?" he asks. Luke whispers: "He's there, he's there. He's the one *on the Cross!*"

Now don't misunderstand me. It's not that Mark and Paul and Hebrews are wrong and Luke is right. Rather, the reason for Luke's radically different theology of the Cross is to be seen in the situation of the church to which and for which Luke writes. Writing sometime after the fall of Jerusalem in A.D. 70, Luke wrote for a church discouraged, disillusioned, and disheartened. They had hoped that the events leading up to Jerusalem's fall to the Romans were merely harbingers of the consummation of the age, the advent of the Kingdom of God, the return of Christ, the *parousia,* and the vindication of the People of God; but Jerusalem fell, and the *parousia* didn't happen. Many converts to Christianity left to go back into their former religions, Mithraism, the Imperial Cult; and many went back to Judaism itself, after all, they'd been Jews before becoming Christians; many felt they'd never left it. Those who stayed were ridiculed, taunted, misunderstood, and persecuted, especially by the synagogue.

"Jesus the Messiah? Give me a break! He was crucified like a common criminal, and everybody knows Messiahs don't get crucified! Crucified Messiah? C'mon."

For nearly 1,000 years Israel had known only subjugation and slavery. Virtually all their hopes lay with the prophecies that someday God would send His Messiah to deliver them from their oppressors. "When Messiah comes" was the phrase that prefaced all the beautiful stories in Israel. That's what you told the beggar: "Sorry I can't help you, friend, but when Messiah comes, there'll be no more poor people." That's what you told the cripple: "Sorry about your legs, but when Messiah comes, there'll be no more cripples." That's what you told the blind man: "Sorry about your eyes, but when Messiah comes, there'll be no more blind people." Matter of fact, "When Messiah comes" functioned in their world like "once upon a time" functions in ours. "Wherever there's Messiah, there'll be no more pain, no more suffering, no more death."

I know it may sound strange to you, having grown up hearing Isaiah 53 read every year during Holy Week—"He was wounded for our transgressions; he was bruised for our iniquities." Indeed, you can't hear Isaiah 53 without thinking of Jesus, but as T. W. Manson demonstrated in his little book, *The Servant Messiah,* there is little if any evidence that anyone in the time of Jesus ever interpreted Isaiah 53 messianically.[3] The idea that Messiah would "suffer" was simply not a part of the first-century Jewish messianic hope. The belief that Messiah would champion the cause of Israel in taking up arms in a holy war against the pagans was ubiquitous, but "suffering" and "death" simply were not ideas that first-century Jews typically associated with the concept of Messiah.

Luke comes along and changes the theology to say: "Wherever there is pain and suffering and death, *there* is the Messiah." In the Old Testament the term "Chosen One" was technical language for Messiah. Luke alone among New Testament writers calls Jesus "the Chosen One," and he calls him that *on the cross!*

You know why—because, like Luke's suffering, struggling-to-believe people of faith, there are times when what you need, what you really need, is not so much a God who is *over* you or *above* you or *beyond* you as a God who is *alongside* you, a God who is accessible and vulnerable if indeed they're not the same thing, and yes, *mortal,* a God willing go to the gallows for you.

Now don't get me wrong. Neither Luke nor I am saying to you today that faith is somber and joyless. No Gospel makes more of faith's joy than Luke.

Faith doesn't begin with joy, though; it begins on a gallows with suffering love. Next week we'll celebrate the resurrection, but don't ever forget—Luke won't let you forget—that there can be no resurrection until somebody dies!

Luke knows that without the cross, faith wouldn't have much to say to anybody. What would you say to the terminal cancer patient? What would you say to the mother who just buried her son killed in a drive-by shooting on the mean streets of Chapel Hill or Durham or Raleigh? What do you say to the eighty-five-year-old woman, alone, forgotten, in cold storage in some nursing-home where she sleeps all day so she won't have to smell the feces and death all around her: "Smile, God loves you."

No, but I'll tell you what you *can* say. You can stretch out your hands as far as they'll go and say: "Let me tell you about a God who loves you *this much!*"

Bennett Cerf, of the old TV game show *To Tell the Truth,* was one of my favorite storytellers growing up. Of all the stories he told, this, he said, was his favorite.

A little girl whose parents died when she quite young was bounced around from orphanage to foster home to orphanage. She really was a beautiful child, although all the moving and trauma of her young life had taken its toll, leaving her quite withdrawn.

She finally came to settle in a boarding house that was run by an older couple who ran the home not so much out of altruistic concern for the children as for the state welfare monies they received for each child.

Needless to say, they were not very kind to the little girl, and as one would suspect from an experience in such a hostile environment, the little girl became even more withdrawn and introverted. As a matter of fact, she stopped speaking altogether, at least to other people. Her only real friends became the animals that played in the yard with her. A particular favorite was a certain squirrel that frolicked in the tree just outside her window. She would often go to the window and talk to the squirrel as though the animal could actually understand her, and a great bond of friendship developed between them.

One day the woman who ran the orphanage came up to the little girl's room and found her talking to the squirrel through the open window, and the woman flew into a rage. She scolded her severely for encouraging silly animals to "hang around" like that and forbade her to do so again. With that she slammed the window shut and stormed out of the room; but she didn't go far. Rather, she waited and listened at the door to see if the girl would disobey her, and when she heard no sound she cracked the door and peered in. To her amazement, she saw the little girl busy at her work table writing a note. The wife continued to watch her as she finished the note, put the pencil down, and then carefully folded the note in half. Then she got up and left the room with the note in hand. The woman was curious by now and followed her to see what she was up to. The little girl ran out of the house, through the yard, and up to the tree where the squirrel usually stayed. She climbed up into the tree as far as she could, stretched out her hand, and placed the note between the fork of two branches in the tree. Then she climbed down and ran back up into the house. The woman called to her husband, told him what had just happened, and instructed him to retrieve the note. When he climbed down with the note, he gave it to his wife who opened it and read it, and when she did, a strange thing happened. Instead of being outraged by the girl's disobedience, she looked startled and surprised by what she found in the note. Her husband said: "Well, what does it say?" She gave it to him to read. When he looked at it, this is what it said: "To whomever finds this, I love you."[4]

Two thousand years ago, on a dirty little hill just outside a major city in Palestine, between two crossed branches, God hung a letter, and it says: *"To whomever finds this, I love you!"*

If you've found it, then you already know why in the Church we have the gall to call this week "Holy." If you haven't, I pray you will. Please...!

CHAPTER SEVEN

The Moment of Truth

Matthew 14:22-23

L et me dispense with something quickly. It makes no sense at all to say, as some do, that Jesus was who He said He was, the Son of God, and then argue that He could not have done what Matthew claims for Him in this story—namely, to walk on water.

Now, if you want to argue that what the New Testament claims for Jesus simply isn't so—that is, that He is not the Son of God—then, of course, you may believe whatever you like—that this story is legend, nonsense, or worse, out-and-out fraud. If He is the Son of God, as the New Testament claims, then suddenly all other claims that the New Testament makes for Him become credible. C. S. Lewis, in his marvelous, but demanding, book *Miracles* put it this way: "The central miracle asserted by Christians is the Incarnation. They say that God became Man. Every other miracle prepares for this, or exhibits this, or results from this."[1] If Jesus is not the Son of God, then this miracle is no more credible or incredible than any other the New Testament claims for Him. Likewise, if He is the Son of God, then I fail to see why walking on water should be any more incredible than healing the sick or raising the dead or feeding several thousand people with five loaves and two fish or calming a storm. What simply cannot be defended is the position that wants to have it both ways, to hold onto the Incarnation with one hand and to deny the credibility of only *certain* miracles on the other.

That's not what troubles me about this story. What raises a question for me is not the miracle itself but rather why Jesus tells the disciples to get into the boat and go on without Him. Why the distance between Jesus and

57

the disciples? I mean, you've read the gospels. From the time Jesus calls these men to follow Him and to join His itinerant ministry of Kingdom proclamation, the disciples are with Him almost incessantly. It may be an overstatement, but just a bit, to say that the gospel is as much the *disciple's* story as Jesus'!

This is especially true of Matthew's gospel. In fact, Matthew portrays them not so much as Jesus' students or helpers as *extensions* of Jesus' ministry. Matthew's description of the call of the Twelve in chapter ten is much more dramatic and specific than Mark's or Luke's counterpart. Matthew says that the Twelve are given the authority to act in Jesus' name, preaching, teaching, healing, exorcising demons, raising the dead. Indeed, for Matthew's gospel, discipleship as the authoritative extension of the ministry of Jesus is such an overriding concern that you could say that it is *the issue* of this gospel. Then why the distance here?

We would have expected it from Mark. There is a growing distance between Jesus and the disciples in Mark's gospel, a distance marked by failure and fear and misunderstanding and finally betrayal and abandonment—"And they left him, every last one of them!" In Mark, the disciples don't understand Jesus; they fear Jesus; they disappoint Him and even oppose Him. In Mark's gospel Jesus has to say to Simon Peter, the preeminent disciple, "Get behind me, Satan! You're not thinking the way God thinks; you're thinking the way men think!" When you read Mark, you're not sure whose side these guys are on!

Matthew goes to great lengths to redeem the disciples' tarnished reputation. At Caesarea Philippi, according to Mark, when Peter confessed Jesus as the Messiah, Jesus told Peter to "Get behind me, Satan!" Listen to Matthew, though: "Blessed are you Simon bar Jona; flesh and blood did not reveal this to you, and I tell you that you are Peter and upon this rock I'll build my church and the gates of hell will not prevail against it!" Some difference, huh!

For Matthew, the disciples are the representatives of the church in the generation after Jesus, continuing and even expanding His ministry. He softens Mark's shrill description of the disciples. He blunts his criticism of them everywhere he can.

That's why this distance is so strange. Listen to the language: "Then he *made* the disciples get into the boat and go on ahead of him to the other side." The word in the Greek means to force, compel. Why?

Well, I don't know, and I don't know who knows. If John's version of this story is any clue, it may have been because Jesus saw trouble brewing and wanted to insulate the disciples from it. This story, you will recall, takes place immediately after Jesus fed the multitude with the five loaves and two fish. For Jews, that miracle had special significance. You see, they believed that when the Messiah came, he would repeat the miracles of Moses in the wilderness, such as feeding the people with manna from heaven. When Jesus fed the multitude, many of them believed that it was a manifestation of the Messiah's presence among them, and, according to John, many of the people rushed Jesus to "take him by force to make him king!" Did Jesus send them away because He was trying to protect the disciples from this kind of politicizing of the Kingdom of God? Maybe that was it. I don't know.

Maybe it was just Matthew's way of reminding us that even in the best and closest of relationships there's always some distance. Matthew's very honest about disagreements in the church. It's Matthew, you remember, who talks about how the church should deal with "a brother who sins," a clear recognition that even in the church sometimes there's distance. Peter was not only Jesus' lead disciple, he was His best friend; yet you feel the anguish in Peter's voice when in this gospel he asks Jesus: "Lo, we've left everything and followed you. What then shall we have?" Maybe that was it. I don't know.

Then again, it just may have been Matthew's way of reminding his church, and ours, that their experience with Jesus would not always take the form of physical presence, but that sooner or later their experience of Jesus was going to be of the absence of Jesus. "Then, he made the disciples get into the boat and go on ahead without him." That certainly was the experience of Matthew's church, and remember, in Matthew the disciples are the representatives of the later church. It was the number one problem of the Early Church, the absence of Jesus' physical presence. What should they do? Should they continue on without him? Should they await the coming of another Messiah? What should they do? All the gospels deal with it. Luke and John deal with it in terms of the coming of the Holy Spirit. "I must go away, but I will not leave you orphaned; I will send my Comforter, my Paraclete, and He will teach you all things." Matthew deals with it in terms of *faith*, the capacity to risk everything in the confidence that there is a *presence* in the absence. Do the disciples have faith enough to carry on on the *far side of the resurrection,* without the physical presence of Jesus to sustain them?

As a matter of fact, *this,* not the walking on the water or the stilling of the storm, is the major thrust of the story. It's an epiphany story, a story

about Jesus' sudden *presence in the absence,* more reminiscent of a resurrection appearance than a miracle story. Out of a dark night of fear and
helplessness Christ appears to the disciples. They think it's a ghost and are
terrified until He reassures them. This business of Peter getting out of the
boat and walking to Jesus recalls the testimony ubiquitous in the Early
Church that the risen Christ appeared to Simon Peter. Indeed, John, chapter twenty-one, records an appearance of the risen Lord by the Sea of
Galilee with Simon Peter jumping into the water (but not walking on it)
to go to him!

All this has led some scholars to suggest that this story was actually a
post-Easter story, that it constituted one of the occasions of Jesus' appear-
ing to his disciples that the gospel writer placed back here in the ministry
of Jesus. Does that bother you? Don't let it. A gospel writer's reflections
upon the power and presence of Christ didn't respect the chronological
distinctions of pre- and post-Easter so important to us. Jesus is the living
Lord and the living Lord is Jesus; what He is and does, He was and did.

In some ways, it would be easier to understand if that were the case. The
night has been long, and as dawn approaches they are near despair. Across
the water not subject to laws of time and place, the risen Lord comes. As
a ghost? No, but they think He is and so become terrified. Then there is
the word of assurance. "It is I." Is that enough to reestablish faith? It is
almost enough. Then Peter cries out: "If it is you," confirm it by an authoritative command. Jesus says: "Come." Is that enough to establish faith?
Once again, it is almost enough. Then comes the "moment of truth." Peter
must get out of the boat and trust this ghostly, incorporeal Presence that
beckons him across the water, and it terrifies him!

Have you ever had a "moment of truth" like this? It's frightening. It can
scare you to death!

What's frightening about it is that to be in the presence of God is what
everybody wants, and it's what everybody doesn't want. Rudolf Otto, in his
book *The Idea of the Holy,* called it *mysterium tremendum et fascinans,*
the "mystery that both terrifies and fascinates!"[2] It's fascinating because
more than anything else in the world, we want this! It's terrifying because
the Light at the altar is different from every other light in the world. In the
dim lamps of this world, we can compare ourselves with each other, and
all of us come off looking pretty good. We convince ourselves that God
grades on the curve, that all opinions are equally valid. "Well, you've got
your idea and I've got mine, and who's to say?" Then you come in the presence of God, and you're at the altar, and it's all different—"moment of

truth." The whining is over. There's no way to modulate the human voice to make a whine acceptable. The whining is over. The excusing is over— "It's not my fault, it's the school, it's the church, it's the board, it's the government." In the presence of God, all that's over. It just stops.

You know what the moment of truth is. Oh, I know that some people live in the fast lane, thinking they can avoid their moment of truth by filling their lives so full that they don't have time to think about it, but it doesn't work. Like skipping a rock across the water, sooner or later it slows down, and boom—moment of truth.

A man came to Jesus one day whom the Bible calls a "rich, young, ruler." Now, if that's not a definition of American success, I don't know what is! Something was missing, though. He humbled himself before the Nazarene and said: "I'd trade it all for the presence of God in my life!"

Jesus said: "Really...?"

Moment of truth!

They come to us all, these moments of truth, sometimes in an afternoon when you spend time in the monastery of your mind, sometimes, like Peter, in some violent exchange out on the sea in a raging storm of life; but they come.

Glen Adsett, a missionary to China during the communist takeover, was under house arrest when the soldiers came one day and said: "You can return to America." They were celebrating, and the soldiers said: "You can take 200 pounds with you." Well, they'd been there for years. 200 pounds. They got the scales, and started the family argument—two children, wife, husband. Must have this vase. Well, this is a new typewriter. What about my books? What about this? They weighed everything and took it off and weighed this and took it off and weighed this and, finally, right on the money—200 pounds. The soldier asked: "Ready to go?" "Yes." "Did you weigh everything?" "Yes." "You weighed the kids?" "The kids? Why, no!" "Weigh the kids." In a moment, typewriter and vase and books and all became junk.[3] Junk! It happens. Moment of truth.

Fred Craddock tells a story about an incident that happened when he was pastoring in Tennessee. It seems that there was a little girl, about seven years old, who came to Sunday School and church regularly. Her parents never came with her, never brought her; they just dropped her off in front of the church and drove on. They had moved in there from New Jersey with the new chemical plant. He was upwardly mobile; they were both very ambitious, and they didn't come to church. There wasn't really any need for that; no one there could help further his career, I suppose.

On Saturday nights, the whole town knew of their parties. They gave parties, not for entertainment, but as part of the upwardly mobile thing. That determined who was invited—the right people, the one just above, finally on up to the boss. Those parties were full of drinking and wild and vulgar things. Everybody in that town knew; but there every Sunday was that beautiful little girl.

One Sunday, Craddock looked out, and she was there, and he thought: "Well, she's with her friends"; but there in the service, sitting next to that little girl were Mom and Dad.

At the close of the service, when Craddock gave the invitation to discipleship, like getting out of a boat on the water, out they stepped into the aisle of that church. They came down front and confessed faith in Christ.

Afterward, Craddock said: "What prompted this?" They said: "Well, do you know about our parties?" Craddock said: "Yeah, I know about the parties." They said: "Well, we had one last night again, and it got a little loud, and it got a little rough, and there was too much drinking. We awakened our daughter, and she came downstairs, and she was on about the third step. She saw that we were eating and drinking, and she said: 'Oh, can I have the blessing? God is great, God is good, let us thank him for our food. Good night, everybody.' She went back upstairs."

"Silence. Then someone said: 'Oh my land, look at the time. I can't believe it's this late. I guess we'd better be going. Did we bring coats...?' Awkward goodbyes were hastily spoken at the door, and within two minutes the room was empty."

Mr. and Mrs. Mom and Dad are picking up crumpled napkins and wasted and spilled peanuts and half-eaten sandwiches and taking empty glasses to the kitchen. They meet at the sink, and they look at each other, and he says what they're both thinking: "My God, what are we doing?"[4]

Moment of truth.

They come to all of us, these moments of truth, when faith can no longer remain an intellectual "option" or some vague, warm, fuzzy feeling by means of which we justify anything we choose. Sooner or later, it's just you and Jesus, alone out on the water, and you believe or you don't believe, you walk or you sink.

Ever had a moment of truth? If you haven't, you will, because the only way to get from here to there is to cross the water.

Well, that's not really true. You can stay in the boat, but you won't find Jesus there.

CHAPTER EIGHT[1]

Angels We
Have Heard Nearby

Luke 1:26-38

In his amazing book of short stories called *White People*, Allan Gurganus tells the story of an old woman, a widow whose sons now live far away, standing at the sink early one morning dressed in a tatty robe doing the dishes she left from the night before. She's gazing out the window while she does the dishes, looking everywhere and nowhere, when she happens to notice, out of the corner of her eye, something fall to the ground in her backyard. There out near the picnic table lies something white, with wings, shivering as though it were cold. It wasn't.

"No way," she says, but when she looks again, there it is, plain as day, resting on its side on a bright air mattress of its own wings.

"Outer feathers are tough quills, broad at bottom as rowboat oars. The whole left wing bends far under. It looks hurt."

Though her arthritis slows her a bit, she hurries—if you can call it that—outside to investigate. She stoops, creaky, over what can only be a young angel, unconscious.

Quickly, she checks overhead, ready for what—some TV news crew in a helicopter? She sees only a sky of the usual size, a Tuesday sky stretched between weekends. She allows herself to touch this thing's white forehead. She gets a mild electric shock. Then, oddly, her tickled finger joints stop aching. They've hurt so long. A practical person, she quickly cures her other hand. The angel grunts but sounds pleased. His temperature's 150 degrees, easy—but for him, this seems somehow normal. "Poor thing," she says, and carefully pulls his heavy curly head into

63

her lap. The head hums like a phone knocked off its cradle. She scans for neighbors, hoping they'll come out, wishing they wouldn't—both.

As her courage grows, she touches his skin. Feels hard and rough, like an ice tray that clings to everything it touches. She also notices that with every touch, thirty-year-old pains leave her. Emboldened, she whispers to him her private woes: the Medicare cuts, the sons too busy to come by, the daughters-in-law not bad, but not so great either. They too seem lifted from her just by the telling. With every pain healed, with every heartache vitiated, the angel seems rejuvenated too. "Her griefs seem to fatten him like vitamins."

Regaining consciousness, he whispers to her: "We're just another army. We all look alike—we didn't before. It's not what you expect. We miss the other. Don't count so much on the next. Notice things here. We're just another army."

"Oh," she says, like she understands. She doesn't.

Then, struggling to his feet and stretching his wings, with one solemn grunt, he heaves himself upward, just missing the phone lines.

"Go, go," the old woman, grinning, points the way. He signals back at her, opened mouthed and left behind. First a glinting man-shaped kite, then an oblong of aluminum in the sun, a new moon shrunk to the size of a decent sized star, a final fleck of light, and then a memory, Tuesday memory.

What does she do? Who does she tell? Who'll believe her? She can't tell her neighbor, Lydia. She'll phone her missing sons: "Come right home. Your Mom's inventing…company!"

She hears the neighbor's collie barking in the distance. (It saw!)

Maybe other angels have dropped into other backyards, she wonders. Behind fences, did neighbors help earlier ones? Folks keep so much of the best stuff quiet, don't they?

Regaining her aplomb, she bounces back inside to finish her dishes. Slowly, she notices, her joints start to ache again. The age spots that had totally vanished only moments before start to darken again. Everything is as it was before—well, not everything.

Standing there at the sink, she seems to be expecting something. Look at her, crazy old woman, staring out at the backyard, nowhere, everywhere. She plunges her aching hands in the warm, soapy water and whispers: "I'm right here, ready. Ready for more."[2]

An old woman, who seems to be washing dishes, but she's not—she's guarding the world, only, nobody knows.

Seen any angels lately? I have. Well, let me rephrase that. I've seen a lot *about* angels lately, and in the strangest places. Some time ago, NBC television did a two-hour special hosted by Patty Duke called "Angels: Those Mysterious Messengers." Two hours! Imagine, a commercial television network devoting two hours of prime time to angels!

Then there was this feature article in *USA Today* about guardian angels. The story was about the current practice, popular among many, of wearing little guardian angels on their lapels. You've seen them too, huh. Apparently many believe that there's more to life than meets the eye.

Time devoted the cover of its December 1993 issue to angels. Inside, the feature article, "Angels Among Us," trumpeted (sorry about that) the statistic that 69 percent of Americans polled said that they believed in angels.

Not long ago in an issue of the *Ladies Home Journal*—I don't read it myself, mind you, but I know people who do—there was another article about guardian angels, stories about people who, they believed, were miraculously delivered from all kinds of difficulties, people who sincerely believe it was angels who made the difference.

Unless you're hiding under a rock, you'll hardly make it through the Christmas season without seeing yet again the marvelous, if not altogether competent, angel, Clarence, in Frank Capra's classic story *It's a Wonderful Life*.

Frederick Buechner says of angels: "Sleight-of-hand magic is based on the demonstrable fact that as a rule people see only what they expect to see. Angels are powerful spirits whom God sends into the world to wish us well. Since we don't expect to see them, we don't. An angel spreads his glittering wings over us, and we say things like 'It was one of those days that made you feel good just to be alive' or 'I had a hunch everything was going to turn out all right' or 'I don't know where I ever found the courage.'"[3]

Seen any angels lately? Well, the Bible has. Apparently without even the decency to be embarrassed, the Bible speaks of a world populated with angels. Abraham and his aging wife Sarah entertain three visitors among the oaks of Mamre, and they reveal to them that they shall have a son. When the bewildered old couple protests that this sounds too good to be true, the "visitors," angels unawares, say: "Is there anything too hard for God?" Jacob wrestles by the brook Jabbok with an angel in human disguise. Samson's father, Manoah, carried on a conversation with a messenger completely unaware until after the messenger had disappeared that he was talking to an angel.

In the New Testament, angels accompany critical events in the life of Jesus and the Church. They announce his birth, minister to him after his temptation, announce his resurrection and attend his ascension. They assist the fledgling Church at crucial times, aiding the apostles in persecution, assisting with the spread of the gospel to the Gentiles, rescuing Paul and Silas from a Philippian jail.

The word itself means "messenger." *Malach* in the Hebrew, *angelos* in the Greek, and more often than not, that's how angels function in the Bible, as messengers of God. They were not a part of Jewish theology in its earliest development. Early on, Israel had thought of its God as being a very imminent, personal, even anthropomorphic God, walking and chatting with Adam in the garden in the cool of the day.

Later on, this imminent concept of God gave way to a more transcendent idea of God—distant, unapproachable, removed from his creation. Probably under the influence of her neighbors, Israel's theologians posited angels as intermediary beings between God and his creation, facilitating communication between the Almighty and his creatures. They were given special assignments as guides or messengers or caretakers, and certain ones had names, such as Michael or Gabriel. In some ancient texts, angels were thought to be the personification of stars, the heavenly hosts of God, the "army of God" who accompanied him in battle against all the cosmic forces arrayed against the Almighty. In the Book of Judges the Song of Deborah celebrates Israel's victory over the Assyrian king Sisera as a victory of Israel's God YHWH over the cosmic Forces arrayed against him. "From heaven fought the stars, from their courses they fought against Sisera" (Judges 5:20, RSV).[4]

"We're just another army," he said. Coming out of late Judaism, Christianity was from the start influenced by the widespread belief in angels and demons.

It's not at all surprising that when Luke gets to the part of his story where the birth of the Messiah is to be announced to his unsuspecting mother, the "messenger" is an angel.

Across the galactic emptiness the angel flew to a particular province named Galilee, to a particular city named Nazareth, and then in that city to one particular house, to one particular woman sleeping in that house. Her name was Mary.[5]

"Hail!" he said. He whispered it, actually, but angels aren't very good at whispering. Try though they may, their voices sound like thunder—scared poor Mary nearly to death! I mean when an angel appears in the middle of the night in your bedroom and says, "Hail!" it gets your heart going!

Realizing that Mary was frightened, Gabriel said what all angels say: "Fear not." It's the standard line for angels. You get the feeling that part of the basic training for angels includes these instructions: "Now look, before you go, don't forget to begin your speech with 'Fear not!'"

"Well, why?"

"You'll understand when you get there."

With Mary somewhat composed, Gabriel did his job. He delivered the message. "Mary, you've been graced by God, and though you're a virgin, you shall bear a son, and you shall call his name Jesus; and he will be great, and will be called the son of the Most High; and the Lord God will give to him the throne of his father David, and of his kingdom there shall be no end!"

Still confused, however, Mary asked: "How can this be?"

The angel, just as he had to Abraham and Sarah long ago, looked at Mary, smiled, and said: *"With God nothing is impossible!"*

Seen any angels lately? Don't be too disappointed if you haven't. Not everyone believes in angels.

Some biblical scholars disbelieve in angels, at least as spiritual beings. They find it hard to buy into all the mumbo jumbo about ghosts and spirits and angels and such. I have to admit that there was a time when I disbelieved in a spiritual world. Thought it was an anachronistic residue of a more primitive age in which the world was populated with spiritual, incorporeal beings who could pass through solid objects and could suddenly appear and disappear, as angels do throughout Scripture. I thought such a world belonged to fairy tales and children's books with their trolls and enchanted creatures. Having read C. S. Lewis's marvelous book *The Great Divorce,* I'm not so sure anymore. You see, he says perhaps we've got it backwards. Rather than angels being insubstantial and translucent, able to pass through solid objects because they have no substance, what if it's the reverse! What if it is we who are insubstantial and incorporeal relative to their world, and it is they, not we, who are so solid, so dense in fact that they pass through what we regard as solid objects as though they were merely a mist or a fog? "Earth," he says, "is the grey town with its continual hope of morning."[6]

I don't know.

Because the word "angel" simply means "messenger" some scholars believe that angels may not be spiritual beings at all, but anybody who brings a message from God. There is some precedence for this view. The Old Testament book of Malachi takes its title from the Hebrew word *malachi* meaning "my messenger," referring to the prophet as a "messenger" of God. Of course, the word *malach* can also be translated "angel." Was "Malachi" a prophet or an angel?

I don't know, and I don't know who knows.

I know this. Sometimes God sends his messages to us in some pretty unusual packaging, and if we're not attentive, if we're not looking, if we're not listening, we can miss it!

A friend of mine was preaching a revival recently, and because of some pressing business back at his office, he was traveling back and forth to the church every evening for the services. By the end of the week, he was pretty tired.

One night as he was traveling home, he stopped at a convenience store to get a cup of coffee to steel him against the long drive ahead. It was late, and he was tired as he came out of the store. As he walked to his car, an old man came up to him and asked him if he had any spare change he could give him. Well, it was late, and my friend was tired and wanted to get home. Besides, you can't be too careful, can you? Can you? My friend said: "No," with his hands on some quarters in his pocket.

The next night at the church, a lady came up to him and told him that as a result of his sermon the night before she had been moved to give a man some spare change from her purse. She said: "You never know, maybe God sent him my way."

Do you think maybe he was...? Nah.

Even so, I can't help remembering what the writer of Hebrews says: "Don't you neglect to show hospitality to strangers, for thereby some have entertained angels unawares!"

Have you seen any angels lately?

John Duckworth did. He tells a story about Pastor Torgenson who stood before his congregation as they gathered one cold Christmas Eve for a Christmas Eve testimony service. It was their custom in that little church every Christmas Eve to celebrate Christmas by sharing with each other how God had blessed them during the previous year.

As the people gathered, Pastor Torgenson began: "Before the choir sings "Angels We Have Heard On High," let me remind you of a Scripture passage about angels. Turn to Hebrews 13:2."

A tissue-thin shuffle of Bible pages went through the sanctuary and then was rudely interrupted as a haggard couple entered the back. The man had a bushy beard and old, faded clothes. She was pregnant and wore a tattered dress.

"Wonder if they're even married," someone murmured.

"Well, I never," said another.

Old Mizzie Everett just squinted, apparently as confused as ever. Pastor Torgenson smiled and invited them to find a seat. It wasn't easy. The church was full, it being Christmas Eve and all. They had to make their way all the way down front.

Then Pastor Torgenson read those verses, you know, about entertaining angels unawares. He was surprised himself at the timing of it all, this young couple showing up unexpectedly like that.

After the choir sang, he invited people to give their testimonies.

"Anyone want to share a *brief* word of testimony?" He had emphasized "brief" on account of Old Mizzie. My, the way she could carry on about nothing! Trying to remember dates, singing with an awful squeal. Folk just kind of shook their heads chuckled under their breath, and said: "Well, you know Old Mizzie."

Sure enough, Mizzie was the first to the microphone. You could almost hear an audible "ahhhh." True to form, she went on and on, with Pastor Torgenson politely interjecting, from time to time, "Thank you very much, Mizzie," as though that would stop her. It didn't. Finally, finally, she was through.

Then, the haggard young man rose. "I don't know nothin' 'bout talkin' in church," he began, "but me and my ole lady, uh…my wife, we really need a place to stay. I ain't got no job."

When he finished, Pastor Torgenson commented, "We appreciate your sharing with us. I think we can help. By the way, what's your name?"

"I'm Joe. She's Mary."

You could see the wheels turning—*Joseph and Mary?* C'mon now!

"Yeah, I know how it sounds. Really though."

In the fellowship time later, a good number of folks talked with the young couple while nibbling on cookies. Several offered places to stay, and one of the men talked to Joe about a job. Old Mizzie stood in the corner, ignored, sipping coffee and nibbling on a cookie.

Suddenly, she looked at her watch, put down her coffee cup and started for the door. She mounted her three-wheel bike and began pedaling slowly back outside of town. The night air was cold and her old body was so worn. When she reached the edge of town, she stopped near an empty field. The highway was deserted. Only the stars and heaven watched as she climbed the sloping hill. A dog barked in the distance.

"Christmas Eve," she said to herself. "Just like that first Christmas Eve when we sang of His birth. That was easy compared to this assignment! Well, time to go home now."

She smiled, closed her eyes, and reached heavenward. "Goin' home," she whispered, "goin' home."[7]

How's that go again? "Angels We Have Heard *Nearby*?" Who knows. "Is there *anything* too hard for God?"

Seen any angels lately? Are you...are you sure?

PART THREE

HOME

CHAPTER NINE

A Whole New Life

Isaiah 42:1-9

I can still see the shock on her face when I told her that my tradition required immersion for baptism. She had been baptized as an infant in another tradition, but now she wanted to join our church—a Baptist church where they actually dunk people, for heaven's sake!

"Isn't there some other way?" she asked. "Dunking is so...so... inelegant!"

I said: "No, there's no other way. The one thing all of us have in common in this church is that our life of discipleship began with wet hair."

She's right, you know. Baptism is inelegant. Then again, it's meant to be. It means "repentance," you see, and repentance is no fun at all. "Hydrotherapeutic repentance" is what Will Willimon calls it, "and none of us," Will quips, "takes naturally to water."[1]

It's for that reason that when I baptize people, I always begin the service with myself standing in the water, the "humility tank," I call it, and I say:

> When you join the Elks club or the Rotary club or the Lions club, they pat you on the back, give you a pin, and say "congratulations," but here in the church, we do it differently. We strip you naked as the day you were born, put a white robe on you that's really unbecoming, throw you in a pool of water, half drown you, and then, when you come up spewing and sputtering, we shake your hand and call you "brother" and "sister." You know, now that I think about it, that's not bad

73

preparation for life in the Kingdom of God, because the Kingdom of God is a *counter*-cultural movement that sets you apart, makes you odd, and demands that you embrace a will and way and work in the world that is at cross-currents with what most everyone out there believes and thinks and holds dear. It is death...and it is *resurrection*.

It surely must have seemed like a cold, wet bath to Israel too when the sixth-century prophet who wrote in the name of the great eighth-century Isaiah set before the people of God a new way, the way of "The Servant." Since Jerusalem had fallen in 586 B.C., Israel's hope had been that God would someday vindicate his people, liberate them from their captors, and punish the pagans for their presumption in subjugating God's beloved and chosen people. Now, on the verge of Babylon's demise at the hands of Cyrus the Great of Persia, the sons and daughters of Jacob blew on their hands in anticipation of the retribution they knew was coming against their enemies. Now Babylon would find out what it really means to be "chosen" by God.

However, instead of Babylon learning a lesson about what it means to be "chosen," Israel was given a lesson in "chosenness."

> Behold my servant, whom I uphold,
> my chosen, in whom my soul delights;
> I have put my Spirit upon him,
> he will bring forth justice to the nations.
> He will not cry or lift up his voice,
> or make it heard in the street;
> a bruised reed he will not break,
> and a dimly burning wick he will
> not quench.

This was not at all what Israel had in mind! "Chosen" and "servant" in the same sentence? How can this be? It was an oxymoron. No Israelite would ever put "chosenness" and "servanthood" together. To be "chosen" meant to be blessed, special, elect, elite—you know, "the Few, the Proud, the Jews." Servanthood was not at all what Israel had in mind when they thought of their election as the people of God.

In four powerful poems, sometimes called "The Servant Songs," the prophet redefines what it means to be "chosen" in terms of suffering and service and humiliation and death. The message was clear: what power alone had been unable to accomplish, suffering love would do. It was a lesson in "values clarification" for Israel. "God's ways are not our ways, nor are his thoughts our thoughts."

Down through the centuries Israel protested: "But servanthood is so...so...inelegant!" Until rising from the humiliating waters of repentance, hair dripping wet, a Jew, listening for the voice of God in the strangest places, heard him speak again the words of chosen servanthood, "This is my Son, the Chosen in whom my soul takes delight."

Only Jesus, among his contemporaries, dared to relate "sonship" with "servanthood." It was simply not what most first-century Jews had in mind, and yet in the name of God—Israel's God—Jesus dared to put the two together—sonship giving him his sense of identity, servanthood giving him his sense of mission. It was a defining moment in his life!

The church has been protesting ever since: "But it's so...so...inelegant!" It's true! There's nothing elegant about discipleship, because discipleship always begins with repentance, and repentance is a kind of death, and death is no fun at all! As C. S. Lewis reminds us:

> It is something much harder than merely eating humble pie. It means unlearning all the self-conceit and self-will that we have been training ourselves into for thousands of years. It means killing part of yourself, undergoing a kind of death.

None of us takes naturally to water. Then again, repentance and death are not bad preparation for a wholly new kind of life in which lordship is defined as servanthood, and winning is losing, and dying is living.

In his book titled *A Whole New Life,* Reynolds Price tells the story of his personal, spiritual struggle with cancer. It took a tumor running down the length of his spine to remind him of what had always been true: we're all just a stroke or a tumor away from finding out who we *really* are.

"Six months to paraplegia, six months to quadriplegia, six months to death" was the sentence his old life had been given. In his words, he was leaning against a hard wind and scratching for bedrock in the oldest place he'd been taught to look when the light broke through. Lying in bed early one morning about dawn he found himself watching the sunrise not in his bedroom but on the slope of the Sea of Galilee, Lake Kinnereth, where he'd visited twice before. Around him lying in the grass were Jesus' twelve disciples still sleeping. He lay there for a while in the early chill, the light a fine mix of tan and rose, looking west across the lake to Tiberias and north to Capernaum and Bethsaida.

Then one of the men woke and arose. It was Jesus, bound toward him. He bent over Price and said softly: "follow me" and walked toward the lake. "I knew to shuck off my trousers and jacket," Price says, "then my shirt and shorts. Bare, I followed him." Waist deep in the water, Jesus took handfuls of water and poured them over Price's head and cancerous back. Then he spoke once. He said: "Your sins are forgiven." That was it. He turned, leaving Price with water running down his face and back standing there in the lake alone.

Price thought to himself: "But it's not my sins I'm worried about." To Jesus' receding back, Price yelled after him: "Am I also cured?" Jesus turned and faced him and said just two words: "That too."

Price writes: "...with no palpable seam in the texture of time or place, I was home again in my room." Though he was back, he was not the same. That experience in the waters of Kinnereth became for him a defining moment, an ordaining moment, a *naming* moment in which he began, he says, a "whole new life, a life that's almost wholly changed from the old." Still bent, still broken, many challenges ahead, but with a new name![1]

"Behold my *servant,* my chosen, in whom my soul delights."

There's an old, old story I dearly love. It's about two monks, one old and the other a novice, walking together one morning in the monastery, and the novice turns to the saintly old monk and asks: "Tell me, Father, do you still wrestle with the Devil?"

"Oh, no, my son," he answered. "I'm much too old and too wise for that! You see, now I wrestle with God."

"With God?" the young novice exclaimed; but Father, do you hope to win?"

"Oh no, no, no, my child," said the old monk. "I hope to lose!"

CHAPTER TEN[1]

The Presence in the Absence

Isaiah 42:1-9

Some time ago I got home in the evening and found the house was empty. Our son was at football practice, and my wife had left a note on the counter reminding me that she had a commitment and would not be home until later.

"Dinner is on the stove," she wrote. "Your favorite—spaghetti. Enjoy!"

I chuckled under my breath, helped myself to a plateful, and sat down alone at the little table in the kitchen to eat my supper.

I chuckled because she called spaghetti "my favorite." It's an inside joke. You see, when my wife and I were first married, the first thing she ever cooked for me was spaghetti. It was very *interesting* spaghetti, shall we say.

My wife has since become an excellent cook, but it was not always so! She had not done much cooking growing up at home, and those first few meals after we were married were an "adventure," to say the least.

Now, let's be honest. Like any story, the story of my wife's now infamous spaghetti has grown through the years, but it was memorable.

It was another place and another time, but I came home to find my new bride looking somewhat panicked but trying not to let it show, busily stirring some white, stringy things in a pot on the stove.

She said reassuringly: "Just sit down, honey, and read the paper. Dinner will be ready shortly." She said it like she knew what she was doing, so I smiled, sat down, and pretended to read the paper, but a growing sense of dread began to envelop me.

I noticed that she kept sticking her fork into the pot and taking out individual strands of the spaghetti and looking at them as though they were somehow more interesting than I had ever before considered spaghetti to be.

After a while, she looked at me and said: "Uh, do you know how to tell when spaghetti is done?"

I had to admit, in all my years of eating spaghetti, I never once gave the question a single moment's thought.

Then it hit me—something I'd seen my sister do when she was cooking spaghetti.

I said: "Sure!" So I walked over to the pot, reached in with the fork, and took out a single strand of the spaghetti, and when it cooled enough for me to handle, I picked it up and promptly threw it at the cabinets. Plop—stuck right there!

I said: "It's done," and walked back over to the table, sat down, and began to read the paper again.

You know, wives get upset about the *least* little things, don't they? I mean, I thought she was going to kill me!

"What are you doing?"

"Testing the spaghetti."

"For what, *building materials?*"

I said: "Isn't that the way *everybody* tests spaghetti?"

She said: "Most people *eat* spaghetti; you're the only one who *throws* it!"

It was getting dark as I sat alone in the kitchen eating that plateful of spaghetti, but all of a sudden I found myself laughing out loud, remembering that first encounter with spaghetti long ago and far away. It was already too late to retrieve them when I looked across the empty table and let loose the words: "Do you remember that time when we cooked spaghetti…?"

I thought: "This is silly. I'm talking to myself."

I was alone. There was nobody there. As I ate that plateful of spaghetti, though, somehow I knew that though no one was sitting at table with me, I really *was* sharing it!

Did that ever happen to you? It happened to the Early Church everytime they sat down together to eat the Lord's Supper. That's really what this story's about here in Luke—the Presence in the absence.

I know, I know, you thought this story was an Easter story, not a communion story, and it's true! It starts out being an Easter story. Two lonely and disillusioned disciples of the crucified Jesus were walking along on the road from Jerusalem to Emmaus discussing the events of the past few days, when suddenly a stranger appears among them. It's Jesus, but they don't know it.

"What are you talking about?" he asks them.

"Have you been hiding under a rock, or what?"

"No, really, what are you guys talking about?" For the benefit of the stranger—and *ours* too, because we've also joined them on that walk to Emmaus—Cleopas and the other guy tell Jesus and us what's happened. Kind of a "flashback," you know.

Well, it gets late, and so sensing this stranger has no place to go for supper they invite him, *and us,* to supper. Just about the time we all get settled around the table, something begins to happen. What started out as an ordinary meal, an act of hospitality to a stranger, becomes Communion with the Risen Christ!

Look at how Luke describes it. "When he was reclining at table with them…". Did you get that? *Reclining* at table with them—that's what the Greek says. You don't recline at table for an ordinary meal. Only at Jewish festival meals, like Passover, did Jews recline—just as Jesus had done with his disciples just a few days earlier when he shared the "Last Supper" with them. Get it?

Listen to how Luke describes the serving of the meal: "And he took bread and blessed, and broke it, and gave it to them…" Sound familiar?—"took…blessed…broke…gave."

When did Jesus become the host at this supper? I thought he was the guest, and yet, when they join him at Table, what started out as supper ends as sacrament. The presence of the Risen Christ turns an ordinary meal for a hungry stranger into a sacrament of the grace of God.

Luke's point is: *every time believers gather at Table in his name, He'll be there!* He's the "presence in the absence." Notice, Luke says, "They recognized him when he broke the bread with them." Now, Jesus had just spent considerable time explaining to them who he was by interpreting the Scriptures to them, and they didn't recognize him. They didn't have a clue who he was, but when they broke bread with him, bingo! "It's Jesus!" *Then* they say: "Didn't our hearts burn within us when he opened to us the Scriptures?" They most certainly did *not!* They didn't even recognize him when he was interpreting the Scriptures to them! Somehow, the experience at Table made it all clear.

Do you see what Luke is doing? He's reminding his church—and ours—that stories about the Risen Christ alone aren't sufficient to convince anybody of Christ's presence. They actually walked and talked with him, and they didn't know him. They were eyewitnesses to the Resurrection, and yet they didn't know what they'd witnessed.

Neither is the Scripture alone adequate to reassure us of the Risen Lord's continued presence among us. After all, resurrection stories and even the Scriptures are ultimately witnesses to *somebody else's* experience with the Risen Christ. Were that the whole story, all believers except those select few would experience only the *absence* of Jesus, fated to try to keep faith alive on a thin diet of reports of somebody else's experience with him. Luke's church—and ours—would be relegated to being secondhand Christians, living on a "secondhand faith."

At Table he's available to all of us, no matter when or where we live. Even in the absence there's a presence. Can't you feel it? Taste the bread; drink the cup. He's here! He's here! "When he took bread and broke it and blessed it and gave it to them, they recognized him."

There's something about you and me that needs to taste for ourselves to know for sure. Knowing is more than "seeing"; it's also "doing." Father Divine used to say, "We preachers need to spend less time "metaphysical-izing" and more time "tangibilitating." I don't know why it's true—maybe the epistemologists can tell us—but it's true that there is an indissoluble link between "knowing" and "doing." Truth that really is true for me has a corporeality about it—it *smells* true; it *tastes* true; it *feels* true.

In medicine, the dictum is "See one; do one; teach one." I always used to tell my Greek students that you don't really know a foreign language until you've taught it to someone else. We're incarnational creatures you and me; for truth to be true, it must take on "flesh and blood."

The Risen Lord tastes of bread and wine!

It's swimming lesson time. You know she won't drown. She knows she won't drown. You open the car door and say: "Get in, honey, it's time to go to swimming lessons."

"I'm not going! I'll drown; then you'll be sorry!"

You drag her to the pool. She gets into the water, blows bubbles, goes all the way under, sinks like a rock. Comes up spraying and sputtering, looking at Daddy like he's a serial killer.

A week later, there she is, a three-and-a-half-foot little girl about to jump into the five-foot-deep water with her six-foot daddy looking up at her saying: "It's all right, honey, I'll be right here." Splash!

Next morning, 5:15, she's jumping up and down on your bed: "Is the pool open yet, Daddy? Is the pool open yet...?"

It wasn't that she didn't know; it was that she didn't *know!*

His name is Ben. All he can do is smile—can't move, can't talk—he just looks at you and smiles. Ben is the son of a physician who lives in a Midwestern state. Ben suffered an accident when he was two years old. He pulled a cabinet over onto himself, crushing part of his spine. It wasn't anybody's fault! It was an accident!

A friend of mine was the pastor at the church where this physician and his wife were members—good folk—faithful, committed Christians. The first time my friend met Ben was at a dinner party when the physician came in carrying his 16-year-old son in his arms like a sack of potatoes. He looked at the new minister and said: "I don't think you've met our son. This is Ben!" The doctor and his wife had struggled for years with grief and guilt about Ben's brokenness.

As a part of a Bible study he was teaching on the Gospel of John, my friend was working with John chapter 9, the story of the healing of a blind man. It's a little drama, actually, in six scenes, and so my friend, wanting the group to experience the story as a drama, assigned different characters in the story to different members of the study group.

The part of Jesus was read by the physician. He got to the part in the story when the disciples, looking down at the blind beggar, asked Jesus: "Lord, who sinned that this man should have been born blind—he *or his parents?*" The doctor looked at the words he was to read and, recognizing in them more of his own pain than he could handle, broke down and started to weep uncontrollably. Everyone sat silent.

After a while, he regained his composure, cleared his throat, and read: "Lord, who sinned that this man should be born blind? He or his parents?"

Then that Christian doctor read the words of grace from Jesus to his disciples: *"Neither he nor his parents, but that the works of God might be manifest in him!"* As he read those words, the grace of God dripped off of him with a healing and a forgiveness and a grace that flooded that room.

Choking back the tears, he swallowed hard, and read them again: *"Neither he nor his parents, but that God's work might be manifest in him!"*

He finished reading and sat down. No one said a word. No one had to. For in the word of grace spoken to a blind man, long ago and far away, this physician had heard the word of grace spoken to him!

"Neither he nor his parents, but that the works of God might be manifest in him!"

It wasn't that he didn't know; it was that he didn't *know!* Somehow, holding the Book, reading the words, sharing the guilt and the grief, he was finally able to experience the Grace.

We're incarnational creatures, you and me. "When he took bread, and blessed it, and broke it, and gave it to them, suddenly, *they knew!"* "It's Jesus!"

Then he was gone. "Vanished from their sight," Luke says; and they were alone again, sitting at the Table. As strange as it may sound, though they were alone, they weren't *alone* anymore.

A minister in Delaware tells about his own experience with open heart surgery. He said: "Following the surgery, they gave me a muscle paralyzer—didn't want me to move. I couldn't—couldn't speak; couldn't move; couldn't do anything."

He said: "People came and went from the ICU room all day and all night, and all I could do was lie there, immobilized."

"Someone came to see me, and the nurse said to them: 'Ah, he can't hear you. He's in a deep sleep.' I heard every word; I just couldn't respond."

"Then a doctor friend came in to see me. He wasn't my heart surgeon, just a good friend. He leaned over my bed, put his hand on my shoulder and said: 'I know you can't speak. That's okay; you don't have to. I just wanted you to know that *I'm here.'"*

I was sitting there "at table" alone, smiling to myself, eating spaghetti, thinking about another time when I was sitting at another table eating spaghetti—or was it bread and wine? I don't know.

All of a sudden, I had this feeling—*I wasn't really alone!*

Has that ever happened to you...?

CHAPTER ELEVEN

The Gathering

Ephesians 1:3-14

You'll have to forgive me if I'm a bit distracted this morning. This is the weekend that my family, the Stacys, are all gathered down at Lake Placid, Florida, for our annual family reunion. It's quite a gathering! There'll be four generations of Stacys there. Hey, is this a great country or what?

My oldest brother will do the cooking. He grumbles and complains about the heat a lot, what with having to tend the barbecue grill all morning in the hot, central Florida sun. You try to relieve him, though, and he'll say something like: "Does a surgeon ask to be relieved just because he's worked up a sweat in the O.R.? My God, man, I've got ribs here!"

My younger brother will be there. He'll bring the pig—not for the barbecue though. It's a pet pig, actually—a Vietnamese pot-bellied variety he purchased some years ago for the kids. They tell me they make great pets, but when I look at him, I just see him kind of minced with vinegar!

The little ones will play at the water's edge at the lake house. The big kids will water ski and sail. Mostly, we'll tell stories—lots of stories— Stacy stories!

You'll forgive me this morning if I seem a bit distracted. You see, I miss those family "gatherings." It's one of the ways I learn who I am. It imbues me with a sense of "connectedness" and "continuity" that helps to take some of the aloneness out of human existence.

Stories can do that, you know. Stories put value on continuity. They don't place the emphasis on radical discontinuity and juncture, but on

83

the movement within the larger story. I learn who I am and what it means to call myself "Stacy" by fixing my story firmly within that larger story called "Stacy," a story that extends back, not only to me and my brothers and sisters, but to my father and to his father and on and on. That's why, I think, these "gatherings" are so important.

You know what, though, I observe that we modern people don't value these "gatherings" and the stories they celebrate very much anymore, and as a result I think we often feel isolated and "cut off" from things.

In Jay McInerney's novel, *Story of My Life*, Allison is a young woman who lives a "grab all the gusto and never look back" kind of life in fast-paced New York City. Her life is filled with events but devoid of meaning. She has spiritual and emotional Parkinson's disease, a lot of motion but it doesn't take her anywhere. Numbed by it all, she shrugs off whatever life deals her with the quip "story of my life." Her roommate steals her rent money and spends it on a present for a boyfriend: "story of my life." She falls in love with a guy who dumps her for another woman: "story of my life." After a while, no matter what happens to her, she shrugs it off: "story of my life." The quip, and the novel's title, is haunting commentary on Allison's life— there is no "story of her life," just an aggregation of disjointed events without meaning, without purpose, one as insignificant and as empty as the next.[1]

McInerney's novel is a disquieting reminder that it takes more than mere "events" to make a "story" out of our lives. Every counselor knows that. One of the things you listen for when people "tell you their stories" is not just a recounting of the events of their lives, but the significance, the meaning they attach to those events.

Storytelling is a creative act. Meaning is brought to bear on people and events and circumstances where previously there was none, or at least there was not that meaning until you "told the story."

Do you remember E. M. Forster's classic definition of a story? He defines story as the difference between these two sentences, the first being merely a recounting of events: "The king died and then the queen died," the second being a story: "The king died and then the queen died *of grief.*"

You see, there is a sense in which "to be" is to be enrolled in a story, and, as Fred Craddock once put it: "Anyone who can't remember any farther back than his or her own birth is an orphan!"

Now, some cultures still have it. N. Scott Momaday, Kiowa Indian and professor of English and comparative literature at the University of California at Berkeley, writes in one of his books about a formative experience that occurred when he was just a child. His father awakened him at daybreak one morning and simply said: "Get dressed. You're coming with me." Still sleepy, his father took him by the hand, put him in the pickup, and drove to a house on the other side of town. They were met at the door by an old, old, old, old woman. His father handed him over to her with only the words: "I'll pick you up tonight."

He was petrified, but his fear was ill-founded. That old woman told him to sit down on the floor. Then she sat down in front of him, and for hours—all day long—they sat there while she told that boy stories, sang songs to the boy, performed strange and mysterious rituals with the boy.

She told him about how his people, the Kiowas, were born in a hollow log in the Yellowstone River, how they migrated southward. She told him about the great blizzards, the buffalo hunts, the wars with other Indian tribes, the coming of the white man, clash, war, movement southward, Kansas, privation, starvation, finally, Fort Sill, reservation, confinement!

At dusk, the boy's father arrived and said: "It's time to go." And Momaday writes: "I went into that house a boy; I left a Kiowa!"[2]

You see, in the "gathering" and in the telling and in the sharing of our collective story, somehow, in ways I can't even fully understand, let alone explain, it is all of it—all the things we want to remember, all the things we want to forget—caught up, brought back, remembered, blessed, redeemed.

Paul believed that. He opened his Letter to the Ephesians with a long prayer (one long, complex sentence in the Greek), in which he praises God for his "election" (that's the word he uses in v. 3) of the Gentiles into God's family. He does so knowing full well that the Gentiles, his audience in the letter, are listening in as he speaks to God about them.

Then, deliberately employing all the technical language of "election" in the Old Testament about the people of Israel, Paul reinterprets and reapplies that Old Testament language to the Gentiles, praising God, *in their presence,* for his glorious and mysterious plan to unite all peoples, Jew and Gentile, in Christ. In three powerful participles (vv. 3, 5, 9), Paul declares that God in Jesus Christ "elected us" and "foreordained us" and "made known to us the mystery of his will…to gather up all things in him." It's Paul's way of saying: "You know all those marvelous stories about the people of God in the Old Testament? Those stories are *your* stories too! God has gathered a great family gathering, and it was his plan from the start to include you."

In another prayer, written centuries after Paul's, the singer/song-writer Ken Medema celebrates the same "Gathering" with these words:

> We have heard the glowing stories of the things which God
>   has done,
> Of his power and his glory, of his love in Christ his son.
> God of human transformation, for your presence now we pray,
> Lead us ever on the journey as we gather here today.[3]

This morning, we've summoned you to a little "gathering," a gathering to which *all* are invited, and at which *all* is shared—caught up, brought back, remembered, blessed, redeemed.

Come on. Gather round. Hey, have I got a story for you!

CHAPTER TWELVE

God's Geography

Mark 7:24-37

Years ago now, when I was a graduate student at Southern Seminary, I was invited one Sunday morning to be the "supply preacher"— that's what they called it—at a rural church south of Louisville. The gentleman who made the invitation had given me directions to the church over the telephone. The church was located in a small farming community about a hundred miles from Louisville, about twenty-five miles off the interstate. When I told him that I wasn't from these parts and that I hoped we'd have no trouble finding the church, he said: "Oh don't worry. It's real easy to find"; yeah, right—famous last words.

Well, anyway, Cheryl and I started out early Sunday morning heading for that little church. It was a beautiful fall morning and the drive down Interstate 65 was delightful. We took the exit the man had told us to take, and then it started. He had told us to get off the exit and turn left, but he had neglected to tell us that this exit ramp accessed not one but *two* parallel roads, one a state road and one a county road. Cheryl thought we should take the state highway, but I was sure that the county road sounded more like the road he'd described to me. It was ten o'clock and he had said that when we exited the interstate, we were about a thirty-minute drive from the church. Cheryl and I had only been married a few years at the time, but already I had noticed and documented that her sense of direction was hopelessly flawed, and so I said: "We'll take the county road."

She said: "I'm sure you told me that he said to take the state highway."

I said: "When you drive, do I tell you which way to go?"

She said: "So what's your point?"

We took the county road. After about fifteen minutes, the pavement began to run out and we found we were traveling on gravel. I have to admit that that concerned me, but then he'd said it was a *rural* community.

Cheryl said: "This doesn't look right."

I said: "Sure it's right. Just wait. The town'll be right around this next bend."

She said: "If we turn around now, we'll have just enough time to get back to the interstate and take the other road. You know the *other* road, don't you? It's the one *I* told you to take in the first place."

You know, I was beginning to see a whole new side to my young bride. She was so sweet and kind when I married her.

Then we passed a filling station. Cheryl said: "Hey, I've got a novel idea. Why don't you stop and ask directions!"

You know, now that I think back on it, the whole time we dated she never once used sarcasm when she spoke to me.

I said: "Ask directions? Ask directions? Hey, this is Kentucky! Daniel Boone's home state! You don't *ask directions* here! You just keep the sun over your left shoulder and your jaw set!"

About a quarter to eleven, we were deep into pastureland. The only thing living and moving other than us was the livestock out grazing in the fields.

She said: "Well Daniel, don't look now, but I think you're lost!" Smart aleck.

I was fuming. We passed a donkey out in one of the fields. Never looking at her I said: "One of your relatives?"

She said: "Yeah, on my *husband's* side."

It was 11:15 when I finally turned the car around and, spewing gravel in my wake, I headed back. They were just coming out of the church to go home when we pulled up. A man walked over to the car. I got out more red-faced than any farmer there. The man, whose voice I recognized, said: "Purdes called us about quarter to eleven (Purdes, he runs the Sinclair station way out on the county road) and said some folk with Louisville plates on their car just drove past his station and that we'd better go on with the service because the preacher was gonna be late."

Sometimes it's hard to know where you're going. Geography can be important when you're trying to find your way.

Mark certainly believed that. Since the days of Ernest Lohmeyer in his *Galiläa und Jerusalem,* it's been recognized that Mark used geography to do theology. For example, Mark begins his gospel out in the boonies, up in the Galilee, with Jesus preaching and teaching among the rural poor, the isolated and the incorrigible, and then step-by-step takes Jesus from Galilee to Jerusalem, from the village to the city, where the sophisticated and the powerful reside, and it is there, in the *city,* he's crucified. Do you get the point? It was the "up and ins," not the "down and outs" who did him in. Jesus was done in by those whom he threatened the most—the powerful and the privileged.

Again, Mark uses the Lake of Galilee to make a theological point. I'm sure you've noticed it in Mark's gospel that Jesus is forever traveling back and forth across the Lake, from "this side" to "the other side." In Mark's gospel, "this side" is the western side of the Lake, and "the other side" is the eastern side of the Lake. For Mark, there's more at stake here than just geography, east and west. The east side of the Lake ("the other side") is the *Gentile* side, the *pagan* side of the Lake, while the west side ("this side") is the Jewish side of the Lake. When Jesus journeys back and forth from "this side" to "the other side" he moves from Jewish territory to Gentile, pagan territory, breaking the barriers designed to keep people "in their places." "This man eats with sinners and publicans!" When he moved from "this side" to "the other side," he was not just moving geographically, he was moving culturally, socially, religiously, ethnically. Geography in the service of theology.

In today's gospel lesson, these two stories which on the face of it have very little in common, are linked by *geography*. Did you get it when you read the Gospel lesson? Listen again—verse 24: "And from there having arisen he went into the region of Tyre and Sidon." Then in v. 31: "and again having returned from the region of Tyre, he went through Sidon to the Sea of Galilee, within the region of the Decapolis." You see, Mark wants us to treat these two stories as one, and he guides us toward that end by means of *location*. Note: both stories occur in paradigmatic, stereotypical Pagandom—"Tyre and Sidon" and the "Decapolis." From the time of the conquest and settlement of Palestine, Jews regarded the ancient Phœnician coastal cities of "Tyre and Sidon" as the center of paganism. They were the Las Vegases of the ancient world. While he is there, trying to get away from some of the notoriety and attention his actions had generated among his own people, the Jews, he encounters a Syrophœnician woman whose daughter he heals. The Decapolis was a league of ten Gentile cities not under the aegis of any empire, also known by Jews as a place of moral and religious compromise, of salacious paganism and debauchery. Upon returning from Tyre and Sidon, Jesus passed through the region of the Decapolis, Mark says, and while there healed a deaf mute.

It is not accidental that both stories take place, in Mark's telling, immediately after Jesus had argued with the Pharisees over whether or not his disciples should wash their hands, as was the Jewish custom, before eating. The Pharisees had said that their failure to perform the proper religious ritual of hand washing violated the kosher and made them *unclean*, like the pagans. Jesus responded by saying: "There is nothing outside a man which by going into him can defile him; but the things which come out of a man are what defile him." That is, holy is not a matter of what's on the *outside*, but what's on the *inside*. Mark adds the commentary: "Thus he declared all foods clean." These two stories, then, are *cases in point* of the principle Jesus just espoused, and Mark uses *geography* to make the point.

There's more here than that. If you get out a map and actually try to plot Jesus' route in these two stories you'll see very quickly what a tortuous and ridiculous itinerary it is. Notice: Jesus leaves Tyre and Sidon and, according to Mark, "travels through Sidon to the Sea of Galilee, through the region of the Decapolis." Now Sidon is *north* of Tyre, and the Sea of Galilee is *south* of both Tyre and Sidon, and the Decapolis is *east* and *south* of the Sea of Galilee, and yet Mark says Jesus left Tyre and went through Sidon on his way to the Sea of Galilee and the Decapolis. That's like saying that I traveled from Raleigh to Boston by way of Miami and Mobile! It's nonsense, *geographically*. Matter of fact, Matthew, when he told this story, was so embarrassed by how Mark butchered the geography that he felt compelled to clean it up! He just says, "Jesus left the district of Tyre and Sidon and went on to the Sea of Galilee," avoiding the whole problem. Mark's point isn't about *geography*, it's about *theology*. This is "God's geography."

Do you see what he's doing? Jesus didn't go to Gentile territory *for the purpose* of ministering to Gentiles; he went there to *get away from it all* for a while. He finds that even there (and you can't be more "there" than Tyre and Sidon and the Decapolis) God was present, working, healing, redeeming, saving. It's Mark's way of saying: "You know, a funny thing happened to Jesus on his way to heal Israel." It's Mark's way of saying: "If you're going to follow Jesus, you'd better be ready for some surprises, some interruptions, for places you didn't plan to go and people you didn't expect to meet." It's Mark's way of saying: "With God, there are no *detours*, no *side-roads*, no *interruptions*, no *back forties*, not for this God for Whom not even a falling sparrow escapes His attention." Jesus got to the Sea of Galilee by going north when he needed to go south, but that's how it is sometimes with God's geography.

The truth of the matter is you don't know where all of this is going. You don't see the whole map; you don't know the whole score; you haven't seen the entire play, and so you can't tell, *from your vantage point,* what's important and what's an interruption. You might *think* you can, but you can't. We set our agendas, we establish our priorities chafing at every unwelcome "interruption" that sidetracks and detours us only to discover, usually in retrospect, that what we called an "interruption" turned out to be our best and truest work.

My friend, Buddy Shurden, found that out the hard way. He was deep into research for a lecture and didn't want to be interrupted when his secretary came into his office. He let his body language do all the talking. It said rather loudly and clearly: "Close the door on your way out!" She looked at him and sheepishly said, "Oh, I'm sorry, I see you're busy." She left. Buddy went on with his work. Hey, he couldn't be interrupted! He was working on big things; he was working on a plan to save the world for Jesus!

Well, about an hour later, he was still looking at the same sentence in the book, and so he gathered up his guilt and walked out of his office and over to her desk and said: "I'm sorry. Give me another chance to be a human being and I promise I'll listen this time." She did. He did. For two hours he listened to unspeakable pain, a home struck by an emotional earthquake, a woman who had no earthly idea what to do with the hand she'd been dealt. It was all right down the hall from him all the time.[1]

In God's geography there are no detours, no side-roads, no interruptions, no "back forties" inaccessible to His grace. The Christian life is more journey than destination, and the Gospel is that always surprising, often nitty-gritty, stuff that happens to us on our way to somewhere else!

Jesus, on his way to somewhere else, on his way to do something else, stopped long enough to spit and touch a deaf mute's tongue, stick his fingers in the man's ears, hold his silent world nose to nose with his own, look him deep in the eyes and speak slowly, deliberately the most lip-readable word in the Aramaic language: *Ephaphtha,* "Be opened!" and he healed him. The Gospel doesn't get any more down and dirty than that! On his way to do a *big thing* Jesus stops to do a little thing that is a big thing in somebody else's world.

Will Willimon of Duke Chapel said recently that someone came to see him who'd had a really tough time in life. Life had not been kind to this man, and the hand he'd been dealt had been particularly difficult to play. As he sat in Will's office, he said something incredible: "I really believe that everything that happens to me happens because God wants it that way."

Will said: "You can't mean that!"

"Well," he said, "I *do.* Oh, not in any Pollyanna sort of way. I mean that, looking back, even looking back on some of the very worst events in my life, it's amazing to me how well it all turned out. Roads I *never* would have chosen to take turned out to be just the path I needed to follow. It's beautiful where it's all led."

Then he said, "You know, it's as if some unseen hand has guided me to where I would never have gone if left to my own devices, carefully, gracefully, relentlessly leading me home."

It's strange, isn't it. Sometimes the longest way around turns out to be the shortest way home.

There's a name for that, you know. You know what you call that? You know what that's called? *Faith*—it's called faith, the indefatigable confidence that God's geography, no matter how tortured it may appear, unfailingly, relentlessly, everlastingly leads us home.

That's because there is a secret signature down in the lower, right-hand corner of your life. It says "God." He is your source. He is your destiny. He is your soul's secret signature, because you were not only made *by* God; you were made *for* God.

Brothers and Sisters, on this journey we call "life," let me tell you all the truth I know. Live simply, work faithfully, speak truthfully, love graciously, give generously, pray daily, worship regularly—but most of all, keep your heart headed home.

Notes

INTRODUCTION

1. C. S. Lewis, *Mere Christianity,* rpt. (New York: Macmillan Publishing Company, Inc., 1981), 114.
2. C. S. Lewis, T*he Problem of Pain*, rpt. (New York: Macmillan Paperbacks Edition, 1978), 146.
3. Ibid., 147.
4. Ibid., 150.
5. C. S. Lewis, *The Screwtape Letters,* rev. ed. (Chicago: Lord and King Associates, Inc., 1976), 144.
6. Billy Joel, *The River of Dreams,* Impulsive Music (ASCAP), 1992.
7. Quoted in Susan Ketchin, *The Christ-Haunted Landscape: Faith and Doubt in Southern Fiction* (Jackson, MS: University Press of Mississippi, 1994), xi.
8. Frederick Buechner, *The Hungering Dark* (New York: The Seabury Press, 1981), 115.
9. C. S. Lewis, *Surprised By Joy* (New York: Harcourt Brace Jovanovich, 1955), 228.
10. C. S. Lewis, *Miracles,* rpt. (New York: Macmillan Publishing Co., Inc., 1978), 93-94.

CHAPTER ONE

1. This sermon is an adaptation of my chapter in the book *Interpreting Amos for Preaching and Teaching,* edited by Cecil P. Staton, Jr. (Macon, GA: Smyth & Helwys Publishing Company, 1995), 97-114.
2. Shel Silverstein, *Where the Sidewalk Ends* (New York: Harper & Row, 1974), 166.

CHAPTER TWO

1. Frederick Buechner, *A Room Called Remember: Uncollected Pieces* (San Francisco: Harper & Row, 1984), 95-96.

CHAPTER THREE

1. C. S. Lewis, *Miracles,* 153.
2. Heather Elkins, sermon for Transfiguration Sunday, in the *Abingdon Preacher's Annual,* ed. by John K. Bergland (Nashville: Abingdon Press, 1990), 52-53.

CHAPTER FOUR

1. Robert Fulghum, *It Was On Fire When I Lay Down On It* (New York: Ivy Books, 1998), 7-13.
2. Isak Dinesen, *Babette's Feast and Other Anecdotes of Destiny* (New York: Vintage Books, 1988), 3-48.
3. Ferrol Sams, *Epiphany* (New York: Penguin Books, 1994), 1-119.

CHAPTER FIVE

1. Francis Thompson, "The Hound of Heaven," in *English Literature: An Anthology,* ed. by Albert C. Baugh and George Wm. McClelland (New York: Meredith Corporation, 1954), 1376.
2. C. S. Lewis, *Surprised By Joy,* 228-229.
3. From one of Willimon's unpublished sermons. If this story is in print anywhere, I am unaware of it.

CHAPTER SIX

1. R. Wayne Stacy, "God on the Gallows," in *The Library of Distinctive Sermons, Volume Seven* (Sisters, OR: Questar Publishing Company, 199?), 251-267. Reprinted with permission.
2. Elie Wiesel, *Night,* trans. by Stella Rodway, 25th ed. (New York: Bantam Books, 1989), 60-62.
3. T. W. Manson, *The Servant-Messiah: A Study of the Public Ministry of Jesus,* reprint ed. (Grand Rapids, Baker Book House, 1977).
4. I heard Bennett Cerf tell this story on television some years ago, and I have retold it here in my own words based on my memory of it. To my knowledge, the story is not in print.

CHAPTER SEVEN

1. C. S. Lewis, *Miracles,* 108.
2. Rudolf Otto, *The Idea of the Holy,* rpt., trans. by John W. Harvey (Oxford University Press, 1977), 12ff.
3. Story told by Fred B. Craddock, "Did You Ever Hear John Preach?" in *Best Sermons 4,* ed. by James W. Cox (San Francisco: HarperCollins Publishers, 1991), 15.
4. Ibid.

CHAPTER EIGHT

1. R. Wayne Stacy, "Angels We Have Heard Nearby," in *The Library of Distinctive Sermons, Volume Six* (Sisters, OR: Questar Publishing Company, 199?), 79-93. Reprinted with permission.
2. Allan Gurganus, "It Had Wings," in *White People: Stories and Novellas* (New York: Ballantine Books, 1992), 162-66.
3. Frederick Buechner, *Wishful Thinking: A Theological ABC* (New York: HarperCollins Publishers, 1973), 1-2.
4. For a brief, but excellent treatment of the function of angels in the Bible, see Dale C. Allison, Jr., "What Was the Star that Guided the Magi?" *Bible Review,* vol. IX, no. 6 (December 1993), 20-24, 64.
5. Adapted from Walter Wangerin, Jr., "The Christmas Story," in *The Manger is Empty: Stories in Time* (San Francisco: Harper & Row Publishers, 1989), 29-32.

6. C. S. Lewis, *The Great Divorce,* reprint edition (New York: Macmillan, 1979), 38.

7. John Duckworth, "Angels We Have Heard on High," *Stories That Sneak Up on You* (Grand Rapids: Fleming H. Revell, 1987), 154-58.

8. William H. Willimon, *Peculiar Speech* (Grand Rapids: William B. Eerdmans Publishing Company, 1992), 54-55.

CHAPTER NINE

1. Reynolds Price, *A Whole New Life* (New York: Atheneum, 1994).

CHAPTER TEN

1. R. Wayne Stacy, "The Presence in the Absence," *Pulpit Digest,* Volume LXXV, No. 528 (July/August 1994), 48-52. Reprinted with permission.

CHAPTER ELEVEN

1. Jay McInerney, *Story of My Life* (New York: Atlantic Monthly Press, 1988).

2. N. Scott Momaday, *The Ancient Child* (New York: Doubleday, 1989).

3. Ken Medema, "The Gathering," in *The Worshiping Church* (Carol Stream, IL: Hope Publishing Company, 1990), 800.

CHAPTER TWELVE

1. See "Hope and the Rediscovery of Smallness," *Pulpit Digest,* vol. LXXIII, no. 514 (March/April, 1992), 54-55.

About the Author

Wayne Stacy is Dean and Professor of New Testament and Preaching at the M. Christopher White School of Divinity, Gardner-Webb University, Boiling Springs, North Carolina. A native of South Florida, Stacy is a graduate of Palm Beach Atlantic College, West Palm Beach, Florida, and The Southern Baptist Theological Seminary, Louisville, Kentucky. He also has done post-doctoral work in Jerusalem, Israel. Stacy has been pastor of three churches, most recently the First Baptist Church of Raleigh, North Carolina (1990-95). He has also taught in three Baptist institutions: Palm Beach Atlantic College; Midwestern Baptist Theological Seminary, Kansas City, Missouri; and Gardner-Webb University where he became Dean of the M. Christopher White School of Divinity in 1997.

A popular preacher/lecturer, Stacy frequently does interim pastorates and conducts revivals, Bible studies, preaching workshops, and church conferences throughout the South. He also has written extensively in the areas of New Testament studies and preaching, having published nearly forty articles in both scholarly and popular publications. His earlier book, *A Baptist's Theology,* is published by Smyth & Helwys.

Stacy has been married for thirty years to his wife, Cheryl. They are the parents of one grown son, Justin. The Stacys reside in Boiling Springs, North Carolina.